A2 UNIT 1

STUDENT GUIDE

CCEA

History

Clash of ideologies in Europe 1900–2000

Henry Jefferies

HODDER
EDUCATION
AN HACHETTE UK COMPANY

Hodder Education, an Hachette UK company, Blenheim Court, George Street, Banbury, Oxfordshire OX16 5BH

Orders

Bookpoint Ltd, 130 Park Drive, Milton Park, Abingdon, Oxfordshire OX14 4SB

tel: 01235 827827

fax: 01235 400401

e-mail: education@bookpoint.co.uk

Lines are open 9.00 a.m.–5.00 p.m., Monday to Saturday, with a 24-hour message answering service. You can also order through the Hodder Education website: www.hoddereducation.co.uk

© Henry Jefferies 2018

ISBN 978-1-5104-1703-8

First printed 2018

Impression number 5 4 3 2 1

Year 2022 2021 2020 2019 2018

This Guide has been written specifically to support students preparing for the CCEA A2 History examination. The content has been neither approved nor endorsed by CCEA and remains the sole responsibility of the author.

Typeset by Integra Software Services Pvt. Ltd., Pondicherry, India

Printed in Dubai

Hachette UK's policy is to use papers that are natural, renewable and recyclable products and made from wood grown in sustainable forests. The logging and manufacturing processes are expected to conform to the environmental regulations of the country of origin.

Contents

Content Guidance

Questions & Answers

■ Getting the most from this book

Exam tips

Advice on key points in the text to help you learn and recall content, avoid pitfalls and polish your exam technique in order to boost your grade.

Knowledge check

Rapid-fire questions throughout the Content Guidance section to check your understanding.

Knowledge check answers

1 Turn to the back of the book for the Knowledge check answers.

Summaries

■ Each core topic is rounded off by a bullet-list summary for quick-check reference of what you need to know.

Exam-style questions

Commentary on the questions

Tips on what you need to do to gain full marks, indicated by the icon ⓔ

Sample student answers

Practise the questions, then look at the student answers that follow.

Commentary on sample student answers

Read the comments (preceded by the icon ⓔ) showing how many marks each answer would be awarded in the exam and exactly where marks are gained or lost.

■ About this book

The aim of this Student Guide is to help prepare you for CCEA A2 History Paper 1 Option 5: Clash of ideologies in Europe 1900–2000. This option is worth 20% of your History A-level.

This option is examined through a single synoptic essay worth 40 marks, which covers the entire period of the existence of the Union of Soviet Socialist Republics (USSR), 1917–91. It is vital therefore that you are familiar and confident with all the material covered. This includes the changing foreign policies of the Soviet Union and the western European governments, and also the foreign policies of the American governments from December 1941, when Adolf Hitler declared war on the USA, up until the formal dissolution of the Soviet Union in December 1991.

This unit explores the clash in relationships between the Soviet Union, which espoused communist ideology, and its ideological rivals among the governments in Europe and the USA. It focuses not only on the role of ideologies in foreign policy formation, but also on other factors that helped shape the foreign policies of the USSR and its rivals: concerns about security, ambitions to expand, economic considerations and the need to be pragmatic when making choices in difficult circumstances. It also looks at the role of key individuals in shaping foreign policies.

The twentieth century was a time of profound political change in Europe and this unit offers you the opportunity to apply key historical concepts such as cause and consequence, change and continuity, and similarity and difference, and to assess the significance of major developments in modern European history.

The **Content Guidance** section covers all the topics, virtually in the order in which they appear on the CCEA A-level History specification, Clash of ideologies in Europe 1900–2000. You are strongly advised to have a copy of the most recent version of the specification to refer to as you go through the topics; this is available on the CCEA website. There are six main topics:

- Russia and Europe 1900–17
- Revolutionary Russia and opposition from western governments 1917–33
- The struggle for survival 1933–45
- The search for security 1945–56
- Cooperation and coexistence 1956–79
- Soviet aggression, decline and collapse 1979–91.

You should use the Content Guidance section to ensure familiarity with the key developments relating to the Clash of ideologies in Europe 1900–2000, and the roles of the key players. The information in this section will help you to understand what occurred and to make substantiated judgements as to the relative importance of various factors at play in the unfolding of events over the timeframe covered by the option. It will also help you master the key concepts in history — those of motive, cause, consequence, continuity, similarity, difference and significance. You will be given a significant amount of factual information to consider, together with contemporary and historical interpretations, to support your study of the option. There is a series of knowledge checks to act as a guide to your progress in acquiring the knowledge required. The answers to these knowledge checks can be found at the end of the guide (pages 76–77). Exam tips given throughout are designed to help you avoid significant common errors made by students, as well as guiding you towards improved practice.

The **Questions & Answers** section is an opportunity to hone your exam technique and become familiar with the Assessment Objective 1 identified in CCEA's specification and tested in the A2 Paper 1 History examination. The answers illustrate good techniques to access top grades for this AO. It is not possible to provide sample questions and answers for every topic, so you must be aware that any parts of the specification could be tested in the examination — not just those included in this section.

This guide cannot go into full detail on each of the six topics, so you should use it alongside other resources such as class notes and at least some of the books in the Reading List drawn up in CCEA's specification.

Bibliography

Craig, G. (1978) *Germany 1866–1945*, Oxford University Press.

Darby, G. (2007) *Hitler, Appeasement and the Road to War 1933–41*, Hodder.

Donaldson, R. and Nogee, J. (2014) *The Foreign Policy of Russia: Changing systems, enduring interests,* Routledge.

Edwards, O. (2002) *The USA and the Cold War 1945–63*, Hodder.

Evans, D. and Jenkins, J. (2001) *Years of Russia and the USSR 1851–1991*, Hodder.

Gaddis, L. (2007) *The Cold War*, Oxford University Press.

Goldgeier, J. (1994) *Leadership Style and Soviet Foreign Policy: Stalin, Khrushchev, Brezhnev and Gorbachev*, Johns Hopkins University Press.

Gorodetsky, G. (1994) *Soviet Foreign Policy 1917–1991*, Psychology Press.

Grachev, A. (2008) *Gorbachev's Gamble: Soviet foreign policy and the end of the Cold War*, Polity Press.

Hobsbawm, E. (1994) *Age of Extremes: The short twentieth century 1914–1991*, Abacus Press.

Kennan, G. (1979) *Soviet Foreign Policy 1917–1941*, Greenwood Press.

Kennedy-Pipe, C. (1998) *Russia and the World 1917–1991*, Arnold.

Leffler, M. and Painter, D. (2005) *Origins of the Cold War: An international history*, Routledge.

Lynch, M. (1992) *Reaction and Revolution: Russia 1894–1924*, Hodder.

Lynch, M. (2015) *Bolshevik and Stalinist Russia 1917–1964*, Hodder.

Mason, J. (2002) *The Cold War: 1945–91*, Routledge.

McCauley, M. (2008) *Origins of the Cold War 1941–49*, Routledge.

McCauley, M. (2008) *Russia, America and the Cold War 1949–1991*, Longman.

Oxley, P. (2001) *Russia from Tsars to Commissars 1855–1991*, Oxford University Press.

Peaple, S. (2002) *European Diplomacy 1870–1939*, Heinemann.

Phillips, S. (2001) *Cold War in Europe and Asia*, Heinemann.

Sewell, M. (2002) *The Cold War*, Cambridge University Press.

Todd, A. (2001) *Democracies and Dictatorships: Europe and the world 1919–1989*, Cambridge University Press.

Volkogonov, D. (2010) *The Rise and Fall of the Soviet Empire*, Collins.

Williamson, D. (2006) *Europe and the Cold War, 1945–1991*, Hodder.

Websites

http://spartacus-educational.com

www.history.com/topics/cold-war

www.historylearningsite.co.uk

Content Guidance

■ Russia and Europe 1900–17

Main events in tsarist foreign policy, 1900–17

In 1900 Russia was the largest state in the world. It extended 5,000 miles from its borders with Germany and Austria-Hungary in Europe to the Bering Strait in the east, and 2,000 miles from beyond the Arctic circle in the north to the borders of Iran and Afghanistan in the south. It had a population of 165 million people, many more than any other European country. With its huge size and large population, it would be easy to imagine that Russia was very powerful and a threat to its neighbours. Russia, however, was not as powerful as it seemed.

Russia was ruled by a succession of highly autocratic tsars. Tsar Nicholas II (1894–1917) was a man of faith, patriotism and a deep sense of duty. He was, however, also autocratic, indecisive and backward-looking. Despite his conviction that God wished him to exercise absolute power, Nicholas II was often swayed by people he trusted, most notoriously by Rasputin.

Historians are divided in their judgements of the last tsar. Several Russian historians have formed an 'optimistic' assessment of the economic and social progress achieved within Russia in the years before the First World War. The Russian economy in the early twentieth century, however, still lagged significantly behind those of its European neighbours: its *per capita* output and incomes were much lower, its educational attainment was lower, and its popular participation in the political system was severely limited. In addition, nearly half of the people in the Russian empire were non-Russians, and many, particularly the Poles and Finns, were alienated by the '**russification**' policies pursued by Nicholas II and his father before him. In other words, despite its great size, Russia suffered from a number of profound weaknesses that left it vulnerable to threats from its smaller but more advanced neighbours.

Tsar Nicholas II's foreign policy was motivated by a complex set of factors, though its overriding concern was the security of the Russian empire. The greatest threat came from the Triple Alliance formed by Germany, Austria-Hungary and Italy in 1882. Despite the efforts of Nicholas II's father, Tsar Alexander III, to maintain good relations with Russia's western neighbours through the Three Emperors' League (1881–87) and the Reinsurance Treaty (1887–90), Russia found itself snubbed by the Triple Alliance. The fundamental problem was that Russia and Austria-Hungary had competing interests and ambitions in the **Balkans**, a highly politically unstable area in south-eastern Europe.

'**Russification**' A tsarist policy designed to make the different nationalities in the Russian empire into Russians in terms of their culture and identity.

Knowledge check 1

Why was Russia not as strong as its great size might have led one to expect?

The Balkans A politically unstable area where many different national groups, often intermingled with other nationalities, jostled for power as the Ottoman or Turkish empire was expelled from the region.

The Russian empire in 1900

The Balkans

Russian interest in the Balkans had an important ideological dimension based on **pan-Slavism** and Orthodox Christianity. The Slavs are the largest ethno-linguistic group in Europe and they formed the great majority of the population of tsarist Russia, eastern Europe and the Balkans. Most Slavs in the Russian empire, and in the Balkans, were Orthodox Christians. Many of Russia's elites felt an affinity with the peoples in the Balkans on the basis of their shared Slavic racial background and culture and their Orthodox religion. They felt obliged to support the peoples in the Balkans against the Muslim Ottomans, who had dominated the region until 1878 and held on to a swathe of territory in the south of the Balkans until the eve of the First World War. Nicholas II, as head of the Russian Orthodox Church, felt a personal religious obligation to defend Orthodox Christians in the Balkans against their hereditary enemies, the Ottomans.

Russia's elites also felt obliged to defend the Slavic peoples of the Balkans against the ambitions of the Austrians and Hungarians in the region. Russian interest in the Balkans was complicated by the ambitions of Serbia to create a South Slav state (Yugoslavia) that would encompass the Slavic peoples in Serbia, Bosnia and Montenegro and those who comprised a third of the population of the Austro-Hungarian empire. The Serbian threat to their empire made the Austrians and Hungarians extremely hostile not just to the Serbs, but also to the Russians for supporting them. The Austro-Hungarian emperor, Franz Josef, contemplated war with Serbia to neutralise the threat that it posed to his empire. That was something Nicholas II could not allow — not only would it undermine Russian interests in the Balkans, it would undermine Russia's prestige as a **Great Power** on a par with Britain, Germany and France.

In addition, there was an economic dimension to Russia's interest in the Balkans. A third of Russia's export trade passed from ports in the Black Sea through the Turkish Straits (the Dardanelles) to the outside world. Nicholas II wanted to ensure that Russia's enemies could not strangle its trade with the outside world, as this would undermine its economy.

Pan-Slavism The sense that all Slavs should work together to advance their interests in the face of western European rivalry.

Great Power A power with sufficient economic and military strength to exert influence on a global scale.

Content Guidance

Nicholas II understood clearly that the geo-political instability wracking the Balkans could readily spark off a war in which Russia could find itself having to defend its vital interests against Austria-Hungary and its German and Italian allies in the Triple Alliance. The tsar's primary motive in his foreign policy in the years before the First World War was to prevent the outbreak of such a war.

The key method employed to maintain peace was the Franco-Russian Alliance, which was formed and consolidated in 1891–94. In ideological terms tsarist Russia had much more in common with autocratic Germany and Austria-Hungary than with Republican France. Nicholas, however, hoped that Russia's alliance with France would force the Germans to deter Austria-Hungary from provocative actions in the Balkans. The problem was that the German emperor, Kaiser Wilhelm II, responded to what he saw as the 'encirclement' of Germany with the Schlieffen Plan, in which the German Army would engage the French and Russian armies consecutively in a rapid war on two fronts. That is not to suggest that the 'alliance system' made the First World War inevitable. The fact that there was no general war for two decades following the Franco-Russian Alliance makes that clear. Nonetheless, the division of Europe into two armed camps ensured that any conflict in the Balkans had the potential to escalate very quickly into a war that would involve all of Europe.

Nicholas II strove to prevent the outbreak of war by organising the first Hague Peace Conference in 1899, but he was not able to persuade the other states to agree to disarmament or the compulsory arbitration of disputes that could lead to war. A second peace conference held in 1907 was equally unsuccessful.

The most important method employed by Nicholas II to ensure Russia's security was undoubtedly the building up of the Russian economy. His Minister of Finance, Count Sergei Witte, was an economic planner and manager of rare ability. With the tsar's support, he fostered a massive expansion in heavy industry in Russia. He doubled the length of the Russian railway network between 1895 and 1905, and oversaw the building of the Trans-Siberian Railway between Moscow and Vladivostok on Russia's Pacific coast. He tied the Russian currency to the **gold standard**, which enhanced its prestige and helped attract foreign investment to boost Russia's economic development. Much of that foreign investment came from France and formed an important economic dimension to Franco-Russian relations, alongside the strong political and military bonds between the two states. The surge in industrialisation under Witte strengthened Russia's economy, and thus the tax base of the tsar's government, and allowed the country to manufacture more of its own weapons. All in all, it may be judged that Nicholas II's foreign policy was well conceived for the defence of Russia's interests in Europe.

The significance of the Russo–Japanese War

While Nicholas II's foreign policy in Europe was generally peaceful, the same was not true in Asia. The tsar saw the building of the Trans-Siberian Railway as an opportunity to carve out a Russian sphere of influence in Manchuria in north-east China. Those ambitions brought Russia into conflict with Japan, which nurtured its own ambitions for the same region. Nicholas II grossly underestimated the Japanese and would not negotiate with them in earnest. The Japanese responded by overwhelming the Russian fleet based at Port Arthur in China in a surprise attack in

Knowledge check 2

Why was Russian foreign policy so interested in the Dardanelles or Turkish Straits?

Knowledge check 3

How did the alliance system improve Russia's security, while endangering it at the same time?

Gold standard The system whereby the value of a currency, such as the Russian rouble, was defined in terms of gold. This made it easier to exchange with other currencies tied to the gold standard.

February 1904. They routed the Russian Army in Manchuria in the Battle of Mukden in February/March 1905. In May 1905, in the battle of Tsushima Strait, the Japanese annihilated the antique Russian fleet that Nicholas II had sent from the Baltic Sea to teach the Japanese a lesson. In the Treaty of Portsmouth, New Hampshire (August 1905) the Russians had to abandon southern Manchuria to Japan's influence, and cede the southern half of Sakhalin to Japan. Russia's humiliation at the hands of the Japanese proved to be a catalyst for the Revolution of 1905.

Defeat by the Japanese heightened Russian concerns about security with regard to the Triple Alliance. Kaiser Wilhelm II was anxious to secure a great empire for Germany and this threatened the international status quo. When the British government made overtures to Russia for an Anglo-Russian Entente to help contain the threat posed by Germany, Nicholas II was only too happy to oblige in August 1907. That meant the German-led Triple Alliance was countered by the Triple Entente between Russia, France and Britain. The tsar hoped that the alliance system would deter Europe's Great Powers from any confrontation that might lead to war.

In September 1908 Alexander Izvolsky, the Russian Minister of Foreign Affairs, reached an agreement with Count Alois von Aehrenthal, his Austro-Hungarian counterpart, whereby Russia would accept Austria-Hungary annexing Bosnia and Herzegovina, a former province of the Ottoman empire, on condition that Austria-Hungary would not object to Russian warships gaining access to the Mediterranean through the Turkish Straits. Izvolsky intended that Russo-Austrian cooperation would improve the tense relations between the two neighbouring empires, and satisfy Russian ambitions for the Straits. The Austrians, however, proceeded to annex Bosnia unilaterally without Russia gaining access to the Straits. Coming so soon after the defeat by the Japanese, the Russians were powerless to resolve matters in their favour, especially when Germany intervened on Austria-Hungary's behalf.

The 'Bosnian Crisis' left the Russians humiliated and it undermined Russia's 'Great Power' status. It also upset the Serbs, who regarded Bosnia as rightfully part of Serbia. Russian pan-Slavists felt that the Serbs had been betrayed by the tsar's government by a dishonourable deal. The significance of the 'Bosnian Crisis' was that, should another conflict arise between Serbia and Austria-Hungary, Nicholas II would be under irresistible pressure to act decisively to support the Serbs because of the affinity many Russians had for their fellow Orthodox Slavs, to defend Russia's wider interests in the Balkans and to vindicate Russia's 'Great Power' status. Failure to do so would threaten the very survival of the Romanov dynasty.

The First World War

Kaiser Wilhelm II's dream of exercising *Weltpolitik* was shattered when Germany lost the naval race with Britain. From 1911 the German military looked to *Mitteleuropa*, or central Europe, as an alternative avenue for expansion. The German government aimed to assert the country's dominant position across central Europe and into Asia, from Berlin to Baghdad, and planned to build a railway joining the two cities. The Kaiser visited Constantinople, the capital of the Ottoman empire, and made a point of expressing his friendly feelings towards the Ottoman Turks and towards Muslims in general. He authorised German Army officers to help reorganise the Turkish Army. Such German involvement was regarded as a direct threat to Russian interests in the Balkans and the Turkish Straits.

Weltpolitik The name given to Germany's foreign policy that was designed to allow it to exercise power on a global scale.

Rather than risk war in the Balkans, the Russians persuaded the Serbs and Bulgarians to form the Balkan League in March 1912 to block Austro-German ambitions in the Balkans. Montenegro and Greece joined the League soon afterwards. In October 1912 the League attacked the Ottoman empire and took possession of virtually all its territory in Europe. A second Balkan War followed in June 1913, when Bulgaria attacked its former allies to secure a larger share of the spoils. The war soon ended with Bulgaria's defeat, however.

Because none of Europe's Great Powers were ready for a general war in 1912 and 1913, they joined in peace conferences to ensure that the Balkan Wars did not escalate into a wider conflict. The wars, however, resulted in massive increases in territory for the Serbs and their neighbours. The Austrian military chief of staff, General Hotzendorf, was convinced that the Austro-Hungarian empire would be destroyed by another Balkan League, led by an emboldened Serbia backed by Russia, unless he could destroy Serbia in a war. When a Serb from Bosnia assassinated Archduke Franz Ferdinand, the heir to the Austro-Hungarian throne, in Sarajevo in June 1914, the Austrian emperor, Franz Josef, decided to go to war against Serbia. The assassination provided the justification for a war that was likely to happen anyway — as long as it was supported by Germany.

Nicholas II responded to the 'July Crisis' with proposals for another international conference. Kaiser Wilhelm II, however, had already given the Austro-Hungarian emperor a 'blank cheque', promising Germany's support in the event of war. The Kaiser was frustrated by the failure of his own plans to dominate *Mitteleuropa* and had decided that only through war could Germany attain the 'world power' it was entitled to. Ironically, the Kaiser and his military chiefs were persuaded to go to war in part because they calculated that the economic and military progress achieved by the Russians following the reforms instigated by Witte and continued by Nicholas II's prime minister, Peter Stolypin, meant that by 1917 the Schlieffen Plan would not succeed against Russia and France — so the Kaiser was advised that where war was concerned, 'the sooner, the better'. Nicholas II's last-minute appeal to the Kaiser, his cousin, for a peaceful resolution to the Serbian crisis was ignored.

'July crisis' Refers to the moves towards war following the assassination of Archduke Franz Ferdinand at Sarajevo on 28 June 1914.

The determination of Germany and Austria-Hungary to launch a war left Nicholas II with no choice. His primary responsibility as tsar was to defend the Russian motherland. He was also mindful of his obligation to defend Russia's 'Great Power' status, and the prestige of his Romanov dynasty. The Russian sense of affinity with the Serbs on the basis of Orthodox Christianity and pan-Slavism, which he shared, also compelled him to defend Serbia against blatant Austro-Hungarian aggression. Therefore, Nicholas II mobilised the Russian Army to defend Russia's borders with Germany and Austria-Hungary and, hopefully, to deter them from war. The Germans, however, used that mobilisation as their excuse to declare war on Russia on 1 August 1914. Virtually everyone in Russia supported the tsar's decision to stand up to the Germans and Austro-Hungarians.

Russia surprised the Germans with its rapid offensives into East Prussia and Galicia in August 1914. These proved decisive in thwarting the Schlieffen Plan by forcing the Germans to abandon their efforts to capture Paris, which was only 64 km from the front line, and to divert many of its soldiers eastwards to defend Berlin. Russian soldiers fought tenaciously and desperately, outmatched the Austro-Hungarians and the Turks in battle, and forced the Germans to fight an unwinnable war on two fronts until the tsar's abdication in March 1917.

Nonetheless, Russia's relative underdevelopment told against it. It struggled to provide sufficient weapons and munitions to its army — at one point in 1915 up to 25 per cent of Russian soldiers went into battle without a gun, with instructions to pick up any weapons they came across from fallen comrades. Russian casualties were enormous: 1.7 million were killed in combat, and about another 1.5 million died in prisoner of war camps. By early 1917 the strains of **total war** proved overwhelming for the tsar's autocratic regime. Not only did many Russians despair at the prospect of a war without end, there were severe and growing problems with inflation, food supply and transportation. Prompted by popular unrest in Petrograd, the Russian capital, and in Moscow, members of the duma, Russia's parliament, told Nicholas II to abdicate in what was known as the February Revolution. An interim Provisional Government took charge in his place.

Total war Involved states investing almost every resource—human and economic—into a war, whatever the cost.

The Provisional Government

The Provisional Government struggled to cope with the myriad demands it faced from all quarters, but it was unanimous in deciding to fight on in the First World War. The alternative, to surrender large parts of the Russian empire and millions of its people to Germany, was not something it seriously considered. The Russian offensive in June 1917, however, exposed the collapse in morale and discipline in the army since the February Revolution. The formation of the Women's Death Battalion, which was meant to shame its male comrades into fighting with greater enthusiasm, seemed to many simply a sign of desperation on behalf of the Provisional Government. Lenin and the Bolsheviks, on the other hand, cynically promised 'peace, bread and land'. The Russian Army began to disintegrate, with entire regiments putting down their weapons and returning home. By early October 1917 the German Army was advancing towards Petrograd and there was no effective Russian Army to stop it. In the chaos, the Bolsheviks' Red Guard overthrew the Provisional Government in the October 1917 Revolution.

Conclusions

Tsar Nicholas II's foreign policy was motivated primarily by a desire for security against the threat posed by Russia's more advanced neighbours, specifically Austria-Hungary and Germany. He hoped to achieve that aim through a programme of major economic and military reforms at home, and by forging alliances with France and Britain through foreign policy. He took the initiative of summoning the first Hague Peace Conference. He sponsored the formation of the Balkan League to stabilise that region and to deter Austro-Hungarian aggression there. He worked with the other Great Powers to ensure the Balkan Wars of 1912 and 1913 did not escalate into a war that could engulf the whole of Europe.

Yet Nicholas II's motives were complex. As well as security for Russia, he wanted to defend its interests in the Balkans, which included important economic considerations. The tsar and many of his leading subjects also felt a sense of racial and religious affinity with many of the peoples in the region, especially the Serbs. Nicholas II wanted to maintain Russia's 'Great Power' status in the face of challenges from Austria-Hungary. He also harboured ambitions to expand Russia's frontiers, as many of his predecessors had done over the centuries. His ambitious attempt to extend Russian power into Manchuria in China, however, ended in humiliating failure at the hands of the Japanese, while his ambitions to take control of the Turkish Straits came to nothing during the 'Bosnian Crisis' and again during the First World War.

Ultimately, the tsar's foreign policy failed to provide the security he aimed for, nor did it secure the territorial and strategic gains he hoped for. Nonetheless, he did succeed in ensuring that Russia was not isolated diplomatically in the years before the First World War, and his army succeeded in thwarting the Germans' Schlieffen Plan. There was nothing more that Nicholas II could have done to prevent Kaiser Wilhelm II and Emperor Franz Josef from plunging Europe into a world war in 1914. The war itself proved to be every bit as disastrous as Nicholas II had feared, but the Russian Army fought on steadfastly as long as the tsar ruled. It was only after his abdication in 1917 that Russian morale collapsed and the Germans made significant gains on the Eastern Front.

Exam tip

If the examination question specifies the Soviet era, you are not expected to discuss Russian foreign policy from before 1917. Nonetheless, the pre-1917 period cannot be ignored since it is included in the specification. A wise student should consider the key themes of Tsar Nicholas II's foreign policy and appreciate how his search for security included the build-up of the Russian economy, as well as the forming of alliances against Russia's enemies — strategies that would be pursued again in the Soviet era.

Summary

- Tsar Nicholas II's foreign policy had complex motives. Primarily, though, it was motivated by a desire for security against the threat posed by Russia's more advanced neighbours. As well as security for Russia, however, he wanted to defend Russian interests and prestige, especially in the Balkans, a part of Europe with people with whom many Russians felt a sense of racial and religious affinity. Nicholas II also harboured ambitions to expand Russia's frontiers in Asia, as many of his predecessors had done over the centuries.
- Nicholas II's ambitions in China ended in humiliating failure at the hands of the Japanese, while his ambitions to take control of the Turkish Straits were also disappointed.

- Nicholas II's foreign policy failed to provide the security he aimed for, but he did succeed in ensuring that Russia was not isolated diplomatically in the years before the First World War.
- The modernisation of the Russian economy under the tsar changed the empire profoundly, and helps explain the Russian Army's success in thwarting the Germans' Schlieffen Plan in 1914.
- The demands of 'total war' proved too great for the tsarist system and eventually, in February 1917, Nicholas II was obliged to abdicate. Nonetheless, the Provisional Government that assumed power after his abdication soon realised that many of the problems faced by Russia during the First World War could not be easily resolved, as many Russians had naïvely believed.

Revolutionary Russia and opposition from western governments 1917–33

Lenin's foreign policy, 1917–24

After the Bolsheviks seized power in the October 1917 Revolution, their foreign policy, as devised by their leader, Vladimir Lenin, was motivated primarily by **Marxist ideology** from the political, economic and social theories of Karl Marx and Friedrich Engels. *The Communist Manifesto* (1848) shows that Marxists were inherently expansionist, in that they were committed to promoting '**World Revolution**'. They were convinced that every country in the world was destined to become communist in time, but only after their existing governments were overthrown through revolutions conducted by, or staged on behalf of, their proletariat. Lenin and the Bolsheviks viewed every other government in the world as ideological enemies that they wished to see destroyed in order to facilitate the 'World Revolution' Karl Marx had predicted. Western governments in turn saw the Bolshevik state, and its appeal to the proletariat across Europe to stage revolutions, as a threat to their very existence. Hence, Lenin's foreign policy was motivated by profound ideological antagonism towards the governments of Russia's neighbours in the West.

> **Exam tip**
>
> The motives behind the foreign policies of the Soviet Union and its western neighbours are critically important for understanding this unit, and for judging the success or otherwise of those foreign policies. Aim to show an appreciation of the complexity of these motivations.

One could, however, also argue that Lenin's primary motivation was the exercise of power. He showed a tremendous willingness to compromise his ideological principles in order to hold on to power. In the Treaty of Brest-Litovsk (March 1918) he ceded a great number of the proletariat of the Russian empire to German control. His **New Economic Policy** (NEP) was a rejection of communist economics. His rapprochement with the West from 1921 contradicted his ideological antipathy to 'capitalist' states. Lenin's ostensibly proletarian regime proved to be more autocratic and ruthless than that of the tsars, and his governance cost millions of Russian lives through war and economic mismanagement. A case could be made for arguing that Lenin showed himself more than willing to put ideological motives aside in order to hold on to power.

When Lenin came to power in the October Revolution, he and the Bolsheviks expected that there would soon be a 'World Revolution' across Europe after years of terrible war in which millions had died and the proletariat, in particular, had suffered. Lenin was convinced that revolution was 'only seconds away' in Germany. Germany, where Karl Marx grew up, was highly industrialised, had a large proletariat

Marxist ideology An ideology in which class struggle plays a central role in understanding society's supposed development from oppression under capitalism to an idealised socialist society.

The Communist Manifesto A political pamphlet by Marx and Engels that summarised their views about how capitalism would be replaced by communism.

'**World Revolution**' The Marxist concept of overthrowing capitalism in all countries through revolutionary actions organised by the working class.

The New Economic Policy This policy restored some degree of market forces in order to revive the Russian economy after the impact of years of war and the disastrous effects of 'war communism'.

and a popular and assertive Socialist Party (SPD). It had many of the characteristics that Marx predicted would lead to a proletarian revolution. Germany's economic preponderance on mainland Europe, its large population and its central location suggested to the Bolsheviks that a revolution that started in Germany would sweep across the rest of the continent.

Indeed, for Lenin and Trotsky and other leading Bolsheviks, it was imperative for the new Soviet state in Russia that Germany experience a communist revolution because Russia, in which only 4 per cent of the population was working class, was not industrialised enough by itself to sustain communism, according to Karl Marx's political theories. Trotsky was adamant that, 'Either the Russian Revolution will create a revolutionary movement in Europe, or the European powers will destroy the Russian Revolution.' Lenin concurred entirely with that viewpoint. Hence, Lenin's primary aim was to ensure the survival of his Bolshevik regime in Russia until such time as the expected 'World Revolution' swept across Europe and helped to consolidate Lenin's premature and fragile revolution in Russia.

At the same time, Lenin and the Bolsheviks also aimed to lend support to the 'World Revolution' to help ensure it happened sooner rather than later. In part that aim may be characterised as ideological ambition but, given how vulnerable the Bolsheviks' hold on power was following the October Revolution, it should also be recognised as a defensive strategy. In considering Russian foreign policy in the twentieth century one should not draw too sharp a distinction between expansionist aims and security aims, because even before the October Revolution Russian leaders often adopted expansionist policies in order to make Russia more secure. Hence, while it is true that Soviet foreign policy under Lenin had ideologically inspired ambitions to promote communism beyond the borders of the Soviet state, that expansionist aim was also inspired by the more fundamental aim to secure the survival of the Bolshevik regime.

Main events in Lenin's foreign policy

As a political theorist Lenin had contemplated how he might seize power in Russia on behalf of the proletariat. He did not have a coherent programme of government prepared for when he did seize power. His foreign policy, like his domestic policy, was formulated on an ad hoc basis. His top priority was to get Russia out of the First World War in order to help consolidate his power.

Lenin's first policy statement, the 'Decree on Peace', was issued by Leon Trotsky, his Minister of Foreign Affairs, on the day after the October Revolution. The Decree called on the two sides in the First World War — the Central Powers (Germany and its allies) and the Allies (France and Britain and their allies) — to agree to 'a just and democratic peace', a 'peace without annexations and without indemnities'. That was hopelessly naïve, however. The Germans had no intention of forsaking the spoils of war now that the Russian Army was on the verge of complete collapse. The French and British simply ignored the Bolsheviks as they refused to recognise them as the legitimate government of Russia. It was not until 15 December 1917 that Lenin and Trotsky accepted the logic of the situation they found themselves in: they signed an armistice agreement with the Central Powers and began to negotiate a peace settlement with the Central Powers alone. It was a lesson in *realpolitik*: in the real world foreign policy is determined by power, and the methods employed in foreign policy have to reflect that reality.

Knowledge check 4

Why were western governments so hostile to the Bolshevik state?

Knowledge check 5

Why were Lenin and the Bolsheviks so anxious to see a communist revolution in Germany?

Arguably Lenin's foreign policy was a blend of ideological expectations and expediency. That means his policy was influenced by the expectation that there would soon be a 'World Revolution' that would see Europe become communist — but in the meantime, because of the weakness of the Bolshevik regime, he was willing to act expediently and to use whatever methods might be effective, regardless of ideological considerations, in order to achieve more short-term aims, in particular the survival of his regime.

Brest-Litovsk

Perhaps the best example of Lenin's expediency in foreign policy is the Treaty of Brest-Litovsk (March 1918). Finland, Poland, the Baltic states and Ukraine became German puppet-states. Russia lost 26 per cent of its population, 26 per cent of its arable land, 33 per cent of its factories, 73 per cent of its iron industries and 75 per cent of its coal mines, and promised to pay huge indemnities to Germany. Trotsky resigned as Foreign Minister rather than sign such a shocking Treaty: he wanted 'no war, no peace'. The Left Socialist Revolutionaries left Lenin's government in protest at the Treaty. Yet Lenin insisted on signing it. His priority was to get Russia out of the First World War so that the Bolsheviks could consolidate their hold on power in what was left of Russia.

Lenin calculated that the Russian Army was incapable of stopping a German conquest of Russia, so the Treaty of Brest-Litovsk was simply a pragmatic recognition of military realities. Finland and the Baltic states had already taken advantage of the chaos in Russia after the October Revolution to declare their independence in December 1917. On the other hand, what helped Lenin justify his acceptance of the **'Carthaginian' treaty** was his belief that Germany would soon to be swept by a communist revolution, and that any loss of territory would therefore be temporary. Hence Brest-Litovsk is a good example of Lenin's foreign policy being shaped by ideological expectations, while being expedient in the methods employed to achieve more immediate aims.

Early attempts to spread communism

When the 'World Revolution' did not happen as expected Lenin began to take steps to promote it, while always prioritising the security of his Bolshevik regime. Lenin was constrained by the need to impose the Bolsheviks' control over Russia, which was resisted by an array of opponents known as the **Whites** and **Greens** from outside the Russian core controlled by the Red Army, and by anti-Bolshevik dissidents within. The Russian Civil War, which began in earnest after the Treaty of Brest-Litovsk in March 1918, was a multifaceted conflict that caused widespread devastation, economic dislocation and famine, and cost an estimated 13 million lives. The **'Red Terror'** was imposed to consolidate the Bolsheviks' power within those parts of Russia they controlled. It was not until early 1921 that the civil war ended and Lenin's power was reasonably secure.

'Carthaginian' treaty A settlement in which extremely harsh terms are imposed on the defeated participant of a war.

Knowledge check 6

How does the Treaty of Brest-Litovsk reflect Lenin's expediency in foreign policy?

Whites Russian opponents of the communists/Bolsheviks (the Bolshevik were often denoted as the Reds).

Greens Disparate nationalist groups who fought the Bolsheviks for the independence of their homelands from Russian control.

'Red Terror' The political repression and mass killings carried out by the Bolsheviks to impose their control over the former Russian empire.

Lenin's regime used different methods to promote communism outside the Soviet state. From January 1918 the Soviets supplied weapons and financial support to Finnish Red Guards, who tried to stage a communist revolution in Finland. That attempt failed after only three months thanks to German intervention alongside the Finnish White Guards, who abhorred communism. There were similar experiences in the Baltic states, where the Germans mobilised and galvanised local opposition to Bolshevik attempts to reassert Russian control. Once Kaiser Wilhelm II abdicated on 9 November 1918 and the Germans signed the Armistice that brought fighting in the First World War to an end two days later, Lenin hoped for a communist revolution in Germany. He used the Russian embassy in Berlin to support the **Spartacists'** failed attempts to seize power in December 1918 and January 1919, and continued to fund communist activity in Germany to the extent of billions of roubles thereafter, even after the Treaty of Rapello in 1922 improved relations between the Soviet Union and the Weimar Republic.

Spartacists Radical Marxists who tried to create a communist republic in Germany.

Comintern

Undaunted by repeated disappointment, Lenin did not lose sight of his dream of 'World Revolution'. He established a state-sponsored organisation called the Communist International, usually abbreviated as Comintern, in March 1919 to fight 'by all available means, including armed force, for the overthrow of the international bourgeoisie and for the creation of an international Soviet republic as a transition stage to the complete abolition of the state'. Comintern was headed by Grigory Zinoviev, though it was dominated by Lenin until his death in 1924. Its main policy was the establishment of communist parties in countries around the world to work towards 'World Revolution'. Lenin and the Bolsheviks invested billions in comintern to spread communist propaganda and stir insurrections.

Comintern was not an effective method for promoting 'World Revolution', however. In part that was because Comintern never enjoyed much support outside Russia. Furthermore, Lenin was careful not to provoke the West, for fear that it might commit itself to full-scale military intervention in the Russian Civil War. The security of his regime was consistently more important to him than any ambition to spread communist ideology.

Nonetheless, soon after its establishment Lenin's hopes for Comintern seemed to be vindicated, when Hungary became the world's second Soviet republic under Bela Kun, a Hungarian Communist. Kun's Soviet lasted for only 133 days, however. It had been tolerated by many Hungarians in the desperate hope that Russia would support it militarily in Hungary's desperate bid not to lose any more territory to neighbouring Romania and Czechoslovakia. Lenin promised to send the Red Army to Hungary via Romania, but reverses suffered by the Red Army in Ukraine made that impossible, and on 1 August 1919 the Hungarian Soviet was overthrown by Romania.

Knowledge check 7

Why was Comintern so ineffective in promoting communist revolutions?

Lenin's hopes turned next to Italy, where a Marxist revolution seemed to be unfolding during the *Biennio Rosso*, the 'two red years'. In July 1919 a general strike was called by Italian socialists to show their solidarity with the Russian Revolution. Italy was almost paralysed for a time by industrial unrest. By 1921, however, the strikes drew to a close as factories closed down and workers lost their jobs, and employers backed by the Fascist Blackshirts militia reacted violently to socialist actions. The *Biennio Rosso* ended not with an Italian Soviet as Lenin hoped, but with the Fascist leader Benito Mussolini becoming Italy's prime minister in October 1922.

The 'red bridge'

In April 1920 the Polish leader, Josef Pilsudski, tried to take control of Ukraine. Within a couple of weeks the Poles captured Kiev, the capital of Ukraine. In a massive counterattack, however, the Red Army drove the Poles out of Ukraine and Lenin decided to gamble. He wished to make Poland a 'red bridge into Europe' — specifically with Germany in mind.

He believed that it would be easy to 'crush the Poles', impose communism on them and spark off the revolution he had long waited for in Germany. With French help, however, the Poles achieved an unexpected and decisive victory at the Battle of Warsaw in August 1920. In the Treaty of Riga that followed in March 1921 Poland gained a large swathe of territory east of the **Curzon Line**.

Lenin's ambitions to spread communism outside Russia were repeatedly disappointed, despite the fact that he employed a number of different methods to achieve his aim. Though he managed to impose the Bolsheviks' control over most of what had been the last tsar's empire, his attempts to stage communist revolutions in Finland and the Baltic states failed. His support for the Spartacists and KPD (German Communist Party) in Germany also failed. His attempt to use the Red Army to make Poland a 'red bridge' into Europe ended in humiliating defeat at Warsaw. Bela Kun's Soviet in Hungary lasted only four months, and the *Biennio Rosso* in Italy was another disappointment. After the Treaty of Riga, Lenin and the Bolsheviks had to accept that the expected 'World Revolution' showed no sign of occurring any time soon.

Rapprochement with the West

The impact of total war on the Russian economy during the First World War, followed by the destruction of capitalism after the October Revolution and, from March 1918, the adoption of '**war communism**' and the onset of the civil war, shattered the Russian economy to an incredible extent. By 1921 it is estimated that Russian industrial production had fallen to 13 per cent of pre-war levels.

The major cities, including **Petrograd** and Moscow, were emptied of almost half of their populations. Famine and mass mortality stalked the countryside as Bolshevik requisition squads took not only food grain but the seeds for subsequent crops too. An estimated 13 million people died as a result of the Russian Civil War and the chaos that accompanied it.

Economic collapse was a major concern for Lenin's foreign policy because it endangered the security of the Russian Soviet Republic at a time when it was confronted by so many ideological enemies within and beyond its borders. The Kronstadt Revolt in March 1921 showed that the chaos even undermined faith in communism among those who had earlier supported the Bolsheviks.

Lenin tried to rebuild the Russian economy with a New Economic Policy and thereby win at least a degree of support from the people in order to hold on to power. Lenin sought to improve relations with the West to bolster the NEP. Export markets were needed to get money for capital investment and to get access to western technology.

The rapprochement with the West was also intended to reduce the risk of war with the West while the Bolshevik state remained extremely vulnerable. Germany alone, Europe's other pariah state, responded enthusiastically, with the Treaty of Rapello

Knowledge check 8

Why did France support Poland against the Red Army?

Curzon Line Proposed in 1920 by the British foreign secretary, George Curzon, as a compromise border between Poland and the Soviet Union. It was rejected by the Poles after their victory in the Battle of Warsaw, but revived by Stalin, who claimed the territory east of it in the Nazi-Soviet Pact.

'**War communism**' A Marxist economic policy that involved full state control of the Russian economy, including the production and distribution of food.

Petrograd Known as St Petersburg until the First World War, Petrograd was the Russian capital until 1918.

Knowledge check 9

How did the Treaty of Rapello benefit the Soviet Union?

in 1922. German-Soviet cooperation was explicitly focused on trade, but included secret military articles. Yet the Soviets continued to support German Communists with secret finance. Lenin's rapprochement with the West, like the NEP, reflects his expediency, his willingness to use any methods available to hold on to power.

Conclusions

Despite the compromises forced upon Lenin and the Bolsheviks by reason of the weaknesses of the Soviet state, their ultimate aim continued to be 'World Revolution'. The evidence shows that Lenin's fundamental aim was more immediate, however: to preserve his Bolshevik regime, though he never lost sight of his dream of a 'World Revolution'. This was obviously an expansionary ideological aim, but it was also inspired in part by Lenin's and Trotsky's conviction that the Russian Revolution could not survive without the support of more advanced industrial states, especially Germany. Therefore the ideological expectation of expansion was inherently wound up with their concerns for the security of the Bolshevik state established in October 1917.

Western governments, 1917–24

Given the profound ideological antipathy of Bolshevik Russia towards the governments of all of the other European states, it is not surprising that in turn the western governments were deeply hostile to the Russian Soviet Republic. Winston Churchill, speaking on behalf of the British government in January 1920, condemned the Bolsheviks as 'a criminal regime' that ought to be overthrown. The Bolsheviks' governance of Russia during the civil war caused shock and revulsion across Europe: Churchill declared, 'The theories of Lenin and Trotsky have driven man from the civilisation of the twentieth century into a condition of barbarism worse than the Stone Age, and left him the most awful and pitiable spectacle of human experience, devoured by vermin, racked by pestilence and deprived of hope.'

The Bolsheviks were seen as posing a major threat to Europe because of their advocacy of 'World Revolution': they wanted all of Europe to share Russia's experiences. The fact that the Russian Soviet Republic was the largest state in Europe, despite the Treaty of Brest-Litovsk, made that threat real, and it was amplified by the Bolsheviks' appeal to the proletariat across Europe to violently overthrow their own governments.

In addition, the Allies in the First World War were desperate to keep Russia in the war against Germany, though the **Central Powers** were no less anxious to see Russia leave the war, as they believed that they might win the war if only they could redeploy the German and Austro-Hungarian armies from the Eastern Front to the west. Allied governments had another motive for their hostility to the Bolshevik regime, in that the Bolsheviks renounced Russia's obligation to repay any of the loans from Allied governments that had been lent to support Russia in the war against the Central Powers, and they refused to compensate foreign investors, mostly French, for the confiscation of property and assets seized since the October Revolution.

The initial aim of the Allied governments was to bring down the Bolshevik regime before it became established. Churchill's feeling was 'that the strangling of Bolshevism at its birth would have been an untold blessing to the human race'. At first, the survival of Bolshevism seemed most unlikely: the British newspaper *The Telegraph* predicted

Exam tip

Highlight shifts in the foreign policies of the Soviet Union and the western governments to show a sophisticated grasp of the subject.

Knowledge check 10

In what sense was 'World Revolution' a defensive as well as an expansionary aim for the USSR?

Knowledge check 11

To what was Churchill referring in his speech condemning Soviet Russia?

Central Powers Comprised Germany, Austria-Hungary, Bulgaria and the Ottoman empire during the First World War.

that the Bolsheviks would 'not last a month'. Nonetheless, despite Churchill's strong advocacy within the British government, the Allied governments did not commit themselves to full-scale intervention in the Russian Civil War. They aimed to support the enemies of communism within the Russian empire against the Bolsheviks, and to isolate the Soviet state and minimise its influence on the international stage.

Western intervention in Russia's civil war

The Treaty of Brest-Litovsk prompted the Allied powers to intervene militarily in Russia. Officially they claimed to be motivated simply by the desire to ensure Allied armaments and munitions that had been given to the Provisional Government and were being stored at Arkhangelsk and Murmansk did not fall into German or Bolshevik hands. The move was also designed to undermine the Bolsheviks, however, and to encourage their enemies to oppose them. Britain sent a force of 40,000 soldiers, mostly Canadians, Indians and Australians, into northern Russia and the Caucasus. France and Greece sent soldiers to the northern shores of the Black Sea. Romanian soldiers entered Bessarabia. Polish soldiers attempted to conquer Ukraine. A force of 60,000 Japanese soldiers, followed by thousands of American, Chinese, British, French and Italian soldiers, occupied parts of Siberia.

In all, 14 Allied countries intervened in the Russian Civil War. They blockaded Soviet Russia and many of them provided military supplies to the Whites and/or the Greens, such as the British tanks provided to the White General Anton Ivanovich Denikin. The Allied armies generally avoided direct military action against the Bolsheviks, however, because there was no appetite among their soldiers, nor among the public back home, for a full-scale intervention in Russia's civil war. Within a year most of the Allied soldiers were withdrawn as the Red Army succeeded in destroying the various White armies one by one.

The most important result of the Allied intervention in Russia, and of the actions of Germany until the Armistice of November 1918, was to help ensure the independence of Finland and the Baltic states. Those countries, together with Poland, were regarded in the West as a **cordon sanitaire** against the Soviet menace. The French, in particular, were keen allies of Poland against Russia, as they showed during the Polish–Soviet War in 1920. The Allied interventions in Russia had another important consequence, however: they fuelled the Bolsheviks' paranoia regarding the West. Lenin and the Bolsheviks already regarded the governments of all of the other countries of the world as deadly ideological enemies. The Allied interventions encouraged a very pronounced siege mentality.

Despite the Allies' failure to 'strangle Bolshevism at birth' as Churchill advocated, their hostility to the Soviet state persisted. The Soviet government was not invited to the Paris Peace Conference in 1919, though the peacemakers were to redefine the borders of eastern Europe, often at Russia's expense. The Soviet state was not invited to join the **League of Nations**. The policy of the western governments was to isolate the Bolshevik regime diplomatically and allow it no influence in world affairs.

Coexistence

With the Bolsheviks' final victory in the Russian Civil War by 1921, the western governments were obliged to accept that the Soviet state had become firmly established. On the other hand, it was clear after the Treaty of Riga (March 1921)

Knowledge check 12

Why was western intervention in the Russian Civil War so ineffective?

Exam tip

The foreign policies of the western governments are as significant for this unit as those of the Soviet Union. Give them comparable attention.

Cordon sanitaire A barrier intended to stop the spread of an infectious disease.

League of Nations An intergovernmental organisation established after the First World War, the principal mission of which was world peace.

that the Red Army posed no threat to Europe, and the repeated failures of communist conspirators in Germany, Hungary and Italy reassured the western governments about the threat posed by their own proletariats. The Bolsheviks, for their part, finally recognised that the 'World Revolution' they expected was not imminent. Indeed, they needed western capital and technology to ensure that their New Economic Policy (NEP) succeeded. Western governments were keen to improve their own countries' trade in order to support their economies, which were bogged down in a postwar slump. Hence, both sides realised that some kind of '**peaceful coexistence**' was desirable and they were open to adapting their foreign policies accordingly.

In the spring of 1922 the Union of Soviet Socialist Republics (USSR) accepted an invitation to attend an international economic conference at Genoa, Italy. The conference achieved little, but it allowed the Soviets and Germans to come together to negotiate and sign the Treaty of Rapello in April 1922. The Treaty promoted economic cooperation between the USSR and Germany, and included secret protocols to develop military cooperation between the two states. The main significance of the Treaty, though, was political. It ended the isolation of Europe's two 'pariah' states, and prompted other states to respond more positively to the Soviets' requests for a rapprochement.

After the death of Lenin in January 1924, the members of the Politburo, the policy-making committee in charge of the USSR, tried to form a collective leadership. After 4 years of a convoluted struggle for power, Joseph Stalin, the general secretary of the Communist Party of the Soviet Union (CPSU), eventually emerged as Lenin's successor. Following Lenin's death a series of governments officially recognised the Soviet state: first Britain, then France, Italy, Austria, Sweden, Norway, Denmark, Greece, Mexico and China. Japan recognised the USSR in 1925 and withdrew the last Japanese troops occupying the Russian part of Sakhalin. The recognition of the USSR by many states simply reflected their realisation that its existence was assured for the foreseeable future, and they hoped to secure some favourable trade deals. The hostility of each side to the other remained undiminished, however: British prime minister Lloyd George's remark about trading with 'cannibals' is often quoted. East–West relations remained tense, though temporarily peaceful.

Conclusions

The policies of the western governments towards the Bolshevik state were not very successful. Their interventions in the Russian Civil War failed to oust the Bolsheviks from power, though they did help maintain a cordon sanitaire along the western borders of the Soviet Union. Their efforts to keep the USSR isolated in international diplomacy were undermined by Germany in the Treaty of Rapello, and by many other governments after the death of Lenin. The fact that the Soviet Union posed no serious threat to the rest of Europe after the Poles' defeat of the Red Army at Warsaw in August 1920 had less to do with the effectiveness of western policies than with the weaknesses of the Soviet state.

Soviet foreign policy, 1924–33

Officially, the motives of Soviet foreign policy in the period 1924–33 remained the same as they had been in Lenin's last years. The Soviet government wished to maintain 'peaceful coexistence' with the West in order to build up the Russian

'Peaceful coexistence'
Intended to signify that the communist Soviet Union could coexist peacefully with its ideological rivals.

Knowledge check 13

What made the western governments willing to respond positively to the Soviets' requests for 'peaceful coexistence'?

economy, and to avoid conflict in the meantime. Behind the scenes, however, there was a fierce internal debate among the leading Bolsheviks about the future direction of Russia's foreign policy.

On the one hand, Leon Trotsky, one of the key architects of the October Revolution, continued to argue that the future of communism in Russia depended on 'World Revolution' elsewhere in Europe, because Russian society — more than 80 per cent of which were still peasants — was simply not advanced enough for communism to succeed. He advocated a more interventionist foreign policy for the USSR.

On the other hand, Stalin advocated '**Socialism in one country**'. That policy reflected a Leninist pragmatism in recognising that 'World Revolution', though it may have been inevitable according to Marxist ideology, showed no sign of occurring any time soon. For Stalin, the priority for the Soviet state ought to be to concentrate on making Soviet citizens truly communist while waiting for the 'World Revolution' to materialise. This meant avoiding any premature conflicts with the western powers. Like all the policies he espoused, Stalin presented 'Socialism in one country' and its foreign policy implications as being consistent with Lenin's wishes.

In fact, one of Stalin's key motives was to present himself as the 'heir of Lenin' in order to succeed him as the next Soviet autocrat. 'Socialism in one country' was in part a cynical ploy to appeal to Russians' patriotism by declaring that they did not need foreign help to build a communist society. This went against the disparagements of Trotsky who, as a Jew, was already disadvantaged by traditional Russian anti-Semitism.

Soviet foreign policy aims in the years immediately after Lenin's death were characterised by continuity rather than change. They were primarily defensive. The Soviets looked for international recognition and wanted to create the impression that the USSR posed no threat to the rest of the world. Robert Service, a leading historian of the period, has argued, however, that, despite Trotsky's criticisms to the contrary, Stalin never abandoned the Marxist aim of 'World Revolution' in favour of 'Socialism in one country'. He definitely supported the aim of 'World Revolution', once it did not threaten Soviet security.

Lenin's death did not lead to a change in the conduct of Soviet foreign policy. His Foreign Minister, Georgy Chicherin, a former career diplomat under Tsar Nicholas II, remained in office and succeeded in securing diplomatic recognition for the USSR from several western governments. That policy of continuing to normalise international relations in the short to medium term was an expedient that was entirely compatible with Stalin's 'Socialism in one country'.

The 'Second Revolution'

Despite Moscow's official commitment to 'coexistence', Stalin had no illusions about the continuing threat posed to the Soviet Union by its ideological enemies. In 1928 he launched his multifaceted '**Second Revolution**'. At its heart was a series of Five Year Plans intended to transform the USSR into a modern, industrial and socialist society. These were much more than simple economic plans. They would secure Stalin's authority over the USSR because he could claim to have completed the revolution initiated by Lenin. While he modestly claimed to be the 'heir of Lenin', the scale of the transformation envisaged by Stalin would, in fact, make his 'Second Revolution' more profound and hence greater than that of October 1917.

'**Socialism in one country**' A policy that the Soviet Union should concentrate on building a socialist society internally, while waiting for the 'World Revolution' that Marxists expected to occur.

Exam tip

Demonstrate your awareness of the complexities underlying Stalin's foreign policy, while taking care not to spend too much time on them in the examination.

'**Second Revolution**' Presented by Stalin as the completion of Lenin's original revolution in 1917.

In foreign policy terms too, Stalin's 'Second Revolution' would have profound implications. The Five Year Plans were focused primarily on the 'sinews of war': coal, oil, iron, steel and the heavy industries needed for modern warfare. Stalin explained, in a speech he made in 1931, that the USSR was 50 or 100 years behind the West, and had to catch up in 10 years or 'go under'. Hence, Stalin's transformation of the Soviet Union from 1928 was as much about ensuring the security of the country from its foreign enemies as it was about economic and social change and making his leadership of the USSR invincible.

The Litvinov Protocol

Stalin realised that the Soviet Union needed several years of international peace in order to build up its economic and military strength. Hence the USSR was pleased to see the western powers agree to the Kellogg–Briand Pact of 1928 that renounced the use of war as an instrument of political policy. In fact, Stalin's new People's Commissar of Foreign Affairs, Maxim Litvinov, formulated the 'Litvinov Protocol' to apply the anti-war pact in eastern Europe. The USSR signed the protocol, along with Poland, Romania, Latvia and Estonia in 1929, and subsequently Finland, Lithuania, Turkey and Iran signed also. The Protocol was an effective method of reassuring the USSR's neighbours, and the wider world, of its peaceful intentions. Stalin, however, intended the Protocol simply as a means of gaining time while his 'Second Revolution' transformed the USSR.

Knowledge check 14

Where were the countries that signed the Litvinov Protocol with the USSR?

Western governments

Western governments remained sceptical about the intentions of the leadership of the USSR. A reflection of that scepticism and continued hostility was their decision not to invite the Soviets to sign the Kellogg–Briand Pact in 1928. Nonetheless, thanks to the work of Chicherin, who was something of a conventional career diplomat, and the cautious foreign policy pursued by Moscow since 1921, there was a grudging acceptance of the Soviet Union as a legitimate state. The Litvinov Protocol between the USSR and its neighbours was a reassuring sign that Soviet foreign policy was more conciliatory in practice than its ideologically charged rhetoric implied. It seemed as if international relations had finally settled into stability after the tremendous turbulence generated by the First World War and its aftermath.

Yet Stalin, like most Marxists, saw the Great Depression that affected the global economy from 1929 as the crucial crisis of capitalism that would pave the way for 'World Revolution'. Stalin secretly directed Comintern to undermine the German Socialist Party (SPD) during the Depression, in the hope that the German communist Party (KPD) could unite the workers of Germany and launch a communist revolution. Stalin shared the view of Lenin and the other leading Bolsheviks that Germany was the key to 'World Revolution'. For the western governments, the communist threat in Germany and elsewhere in Europe was a reminder that they could trust neither the USSR nor the communist movements it sponsored in their own countries.

Ironically, when Hitler took power in Germany in January 1933, Stalin reined in the KPD for fear of antagonising the new German government. That helps to explain why Hitler's actions to crush the KPD were so strikingly effective. For Stalin, as for Lenin, the security of the Soviet Union was consistently the overriding priority in his foreign policy, though his policy was never exclusively focused on security.

Exam tip

It is tempting with hindsight to blame the foreign policies of the western governments for facilitating the rise of Hitler, but remember that no one at the time could foresee the future.

Summary

- Lenin and the Bolsheviks expected 'World Revolution' to occur spontaneously across Europe.
- Lenin's top priority was to retain power over as much of Russia as possible, until the expected 'World Revolution' materialised.
- When 'World Revolution' failed to materialise spontaneously, the Bolsheviks attempted to promote it through a number of different strategies.
- By 1921 it was clear to Lenin and the Bolsheviks that the anticipated 'World Revolution' would not occur any time soon, and they realised that they needed to change their foreign policy significantly in order to retain power within the Soviet Union itself.
- Western governments were hostile to the Bolshevik state but, because of war-weariness, did not make a sufficient commitment to 'strangle Bolshevism at birth'.
- After 1921 the threat the Bolsheviks posed to the western governments seemed diminished, and their attentions were focused more on dealing with their own economic problems.
- There was a debate about the future direction of Soviet foreign policy in the Politburo after Lenin died, with Trotsky and Stalin taking leading positions. Trotsky favoured a more interventionist policy to promote 'World Revolution'; Stalin preferred a policy focused on building up a socialist society in the USSR alone.
- Stalin launched a 'Second Revolution', ostensibly to complete the communist revolution begun in Russia by Lenin but actually focused on making the Soviet Union economically stronger in case of war with its ideological enemies.
- To avoid war while the USSR was vulnerable, the Soviet Union declared that its foreign policy aimed for 'peaceful coexistence'. This was reflected in the Litvinov Protocol.
- Despite the outwardly peaceful emphasis in Soviet foreign policy in the 1920s, western governments continued to harbour suspicions about the Soviets' medium- and long-term intentions.

■ The struggle for survival 1933–45

The main events in Soviet foreign policy

Stalin and the Soviet leadership did not immediately recognise the foreign policy implications of Hitler becoming the Chancellor of Germany in January 1933. They assumed, despite his undoubted antipathy to the USSR and communist ideology, that for pragmatic reasons Hitler would maintain the Soviet–German relationship embodied in the Treaty of Rapello (1922) and the Treaty of Berlin (1926), which reaffirmed the Treaty of Rapello. It became clear, however, that Hitler's Germany posed a real threat to the Soviet Union. Stalin made a point of studying for himself Hitler's autobiographical rantings in *Mein Kampf*, and he annotated his own copy of it. He noted Hitler's dreams to conquer *Lebensraum* for the German people in Russia and its Slavic neighbours. He noted too Hitler's utter hatred of what he termed 'Judeo-Bolshevism'. Hitler saw communism as a Jewish conspiracy to take over the world devised by Karl Marx. Marx was Jewish, and many of the leading Bolsheviks came from Jewish backgrounds, including Trotsky, Kamenev, Zinoviev and Litvinov. Stalin was the first world leader to recognise the shocking depth of Hitler's fanaticism.

> ***Lebensraum*** Literally 'living space', but Hitler meant it to signify the territory needed to sustain a much larger German population with all the food and other resources it needed, including oil and minerals.

Most historians accept that Stalin's pre-war foreign policy was focused primarily on security. He recognised that the economic backwardness of the USSR threatened its security in the face of more advanced states like Germany and also Japan, which took control of Manchuria from China in 1931. Hence Stalin's 'Second Revolution', driven by a series of Five Year Plans from 1928, focused very much on the 'sinews of war' (see page 23). Five Year Plans, by definition, required peace. By the end of the second Five Year Plan the USSR's military/industrial complex was much stronger than it had been before Stalin took charge of the Soviet Union, but it was still not strong enough to defend the USSR from invasion by Germany, the strength of which grew alarmingly under Hitler.

> **Knowledge check 15**
>
> How was it that Stalin recognised the threat posed by Hitler before the western governments did?

Collective security

Stalin was not sure how best to counter the threat from Nazi Germany. Once it was absolutely clear that Hitler would never set ideological differences to one side and reach a pragmatic understanding with the Soviet Union, Stalin authorised a dramatic shift in Soviet foreign policy. Litvinov was directed to seek a rapprochement with the West to achieve '**collective security**' against Nazi Germany. The USSR joined the League of Nations in 1934 and actively promoted the idea that the League members should unite against states that threatened the world order by going to war. The Soviets renewed for 10 years the non-aggression pacts signed with Poland and the Baltic states, but Hitler countered by offering Poland a 10-year non-aggression pact, which the Poles gratefully accepted. In 1935 the Soviets formed alliances with France and Czechoslovakia for mutual assistance should they be attacked by a third country, meaning Germany. The French would not agree to a full military convention, however, and the Czechs would accept Soviet aid only if the French assisted them first. In other words, the alliances lacked substance.

> '**Collective security**' The belief that the world would be safe or secure if countries worked together to deal with aggressor states.

Moscow directed communist parties around the world to work with other political groups to form a 'Popular Front' against the Fascists. Stalin's earnest desire for 'collective security' with other European countries was undermined by the 'Terror' inflicted across the USSR in the 1930s, however, as this encouraged many people in the West to regard Stalin as a greater threat than Hitler.

Spain

Stalin actively supported the communists in the Spanish Civil War (1936–39) between Francisco Franco's quasi-Fascist rebels and the democratically elected leftist Republican government. The Soviet intervention in Spain is obscure and controversial but Stalin may have seen it as an opportunity to promote communist ideology and also as a defensive measure to curb the progress of Fascism across Europe.

Faced with the determination of Hitler and of Italy's Fascist ruler, Benito Mussolini, to ensure Franco's victory, Stalin drew back from committing the USSR to the defence of the Spanish republic lest he find himself at war with the Fascist powers before the Soviet Union was ready for war. He was also concerned that Soviet involvement in Spain might make Britain and France more hostile to the USSR, and more sympathetic to the Fascist states. Hence in 1938 Stalin abandoned the Spanish Left to their fate. Robert Service wrote that Soviet involvement in Spain reflects the fact that Stalin consistently did whatever was in the best interests of the Soviet Union, and promoted the expansion of communism only as long as it did not affect Soviet security.

The growing threat from Germany

At the same time, the threat from Germany grew. Hitler's rearmament programme gained momentum throughout the 1930s, and the western governments simply appeased him. In November 1936 Germany and Japan signed the Anti-Comintern Pact, which was directed against the USSR and Comintern, while Italy joined the pact in 1937 and Spain in 1939. In February 1938 Hitler achieved **Anschluss** with Austria, making Nazi Germany significantly stronger. At Munich in September 1938 Britain and France joined Italy in appeasing Hitler by allowing him to occupy the Sudetenland, the German-speaking territories in Czechoslovakia. Not only was the USSR not involved in the discussions at Munich, despite its alliances with France and Czechoslovakia, it seemed to Stalin that the western powers were encouraging Hitler's ambitions eastwards. Munich discredited Litvinov's 'collective security' strategy in Soviet foreign policy.

Stalin promoted Vyacheslav Molotov as the People's Commissar for Foreign Affairs in May 1939. Molotov was the chairman of the Council of People's Commissars (equivalent to prime minister) and a member of the Politburo. His promotion reflected the Soviets' growing anxiety about the likelihood of war with Germany. Stalin was desperate to avoid war while the USSR was still unprepared. Indeed, his desperation was fuelled by a spectacular blunder he made in 1937–38 when he purged the Red Army's officer corps. Acting on false intelligence, almost certainly generated by the Germans, that Marshal Mikhail Tukhachevsky and other senior commanders were engaged in a 'military-fascist plot' against him, Stalin had 30,000 officers discharged from the Red Army, and thousands of them were arrested and shot. It caused chaos in the Soviet military command structures precisely at the time

Knowledge check 16

Why did the western governments not respond more positively to Stalin's calls for 'collective security'?

Exam tip

The link between domestic developments and foreign policy is something you have to consider throughout the twentieth century.

Knowledge check 17

How did the Munich Conference discredit Litvinov's policy for 'collective security'?

Anschluss The term used to signify the unification of Germany and Austria. It was achieved by Hitler in 1938.

when war seemed likely. Stalin and Molotov agreed that in the circumstances war had to be avoided at all costs.

The governments of western Europe never conceived of Hitler and Stalin forming some kind of pact. The ideological antipathy between the two dictators made that seem impossible. Hence, when Stalin made a last-ditch effort to form a defensive alliance with Britain and France against Germany in the summer of 1939, they remained evasive. The British and French did not want to see the Red Army move into the heart of Europe and impose communism in its wake. The French knew too that the Poles would never allow the Red Army into their country, for fear it would never leave. The British, for their part, were confident that alongside the French they could defeat the Germans without Russian help. Nonetheless, to avoid an open breach with the Soviets, the British played for time. They engaged in half-hearted discussions. Under pressure to do more, they sent Admiral Plunkett-Ernle-Erle-Drax to Moscow with instructions to speak to the Soviets but not to agree to anything.

On 15 August 1939 the Soviet People's Commissar of Defence, Marshal Voroshilov, met Plunkett-Ernle-Erle-Drax and his French counterpart in Moscow and offered to deploy 120 army divisions against Germany in the event of war, but the British and French delegations replied that they were not authorised to respond to any offers. When Voroshilov asked Plunkett-Ernle-Erle-Drax how many divisions Britain could deploy against Germany, he was appalled to learn that there were only 16 that were combat-ready, leaving the Soviets shocked that Britain was so ill-prepared for the looming war. Just one week later the Soviets signed the Nazi–Soviet Pact.

The Nazi–Soviet Pact

There is much debate about Stalin's motives because his personal archives have not been published and historians have to rely on official editions of the Soviet archives, which are selective and incomplete. The main debate focuses on the extent to which Stalin's foreign policy was defensive or aggressive. Most historians accept that Stalin's foreign policy before the war was primarily motivated by security concerns, but recently a number of historians, most prominently R.C. Raack, have highlighted what they see as a more aggressive emphasis in Stalin's foreign policy. It seems clear, however, that while Stalin's chief concern was security, he was willing to exploit any opportunity for expansion that might arise. He saw the Nazi–Soviet Pact as offering 'protection and opportunity'.

The German and Soviet governments signed a 10-year non-aggression pact, which guaranteed the USSR a period of peace, not perhaps 10 years but enough time, Stalin expected, for him to strengthen the Red Army sufficiently to make the USSR impregnable to a future German invasion. In the immediate term the Soviet Union would gain control of eastern Poland and have a **sphere of influence** in the Baltic that was recognised by the Germans, while Britain and France would be powerless to interfere.

On 17 September 1939 the Red Army invaded eastern Poland, which was then annexed by the Soviet Union. Stalin forced the governments of Estonia, Latvia and Lithuania to sign mutual assistance pacts with the USSR and to allow the Soviets to establish military bases in their countries, ostensibly to protect them from Germany. In June 1940 Soviet forces seized full control of the Baltic states and established communist puppet-governments in each of them before they were incorporated into the USSR in July 1940.

Knowledge check 18

Why did the Soviets decide to make a pact with Germany after meeting with the British and French representatives in Moscow in August 1939?

Exam tip

The circumstances surrounding the signing of the Nazi–Soviet Pact can allow you to show a clear understanding of complicated developments.

Sphere of influence
The geographical areas beyond a state's boundaries over which it exercises some level of control.

Stalin may have planned a similar fate for Finland, but the Finns refused to allow the Soviets to establish military bases in their country. The Finns also refused to transfer the part of Finland close to Leningrad to the USSR in return for land in Karelia. Consequently, on 30 November 1939 the Red Army invaded Finland. The 'Winter War' resulted in a Soviet victory, eventually, but only after massive losses of men and material by the Red Army. To bring the war to an end in March 1940 Stalin acknowledged Finland's independence and annexed only 11 per cent of Finland's territory, mostly to create a buffer zone to protect Leningrad. The chief significance of the 'Winter War' was that the Red Army's poor performance persuaded Hitler that the German Army would easily conquer the USSR.

Stalin's annexation of south-eastern Finland, the Baltic states, eastern Poland and Bessarabia can be seen as attempts on his part to strengthen the Soviet Union against a German invasion, leading one to interpret his expansion westwards as being motivated by insecurity rather than ambition. Stalin's ambitions, however, were much grander than simply pushing the USSR's border to the bounds of the former tsarist empire in order to make it more secure. Stalin expected the western powers of Germany, Britain, France and Italy to destroy each other in a protracted war very much like the First World War, and thus to open the way for a Soviet conquest of the continent. That would provide a plausible explanation for Stalin remaining neutral while the German Army invaded the Low Countries and France in May 1940: he never imagined that the French and British armies would collapse as rapidly as they did before the German juggernaut.

German General Wilhelm Keitel later justified the invasion of the USSR in June 1941 as a pre-emptive response to Soviet plans to invade Europe. There were indeed Soviet plans to invade Europe, but Soviet Marshal Zhukov later explained how he and Marshal Timoshenko responded to intelligence reports of an imminent Nazi invasion of the USSR in June 1941 by drawing up contingency plans for a pre-emptive strike on the Germans, without Stalin's authorisation. Without full access to Stalin's personal archives it remains extremely difficult to determine precisely what Stalin's intentions were in signing the Nazi–Soviet Pact and over the following 2 years. Undoubtedly, his anxiety to avoid war in the short term was a key consideration. It seems clear too, however, that the pact reflected Stalin's ambitions, which had been suppressed while he transformed the Soviet Union and built up its defences. Within 10 months of signing the Pact, Stalin had pushed the borders of the USSR westwards, virtually to where they had been under Tsar Nicholas II, except in Finland where military setbacks may have forced him to restrict his ambitions.

It is entirely plausible that Stalin hoped the Second World War would facilitate the 'World Revolution' that he expected, or would at least allow the Red Army to impose his will on an exhausted Europe. It cannot be proved that Stalin planned to invade Europe in 1941, but it can be concluded that Stalin saw no reason why his foreign policies could not provide 'protection and opportunity' — that is, ensure the security of the Soviet Union and facilitate his ideologically inspired ambitions. That dualism was a consistent thread in Soviet foreign policy.

The Great Patriotic War

Between the signing of the Nazi–Soviet Pact in August 1939 and **Operation Barbarossa** in June 1941, the Red Army increased in size from 2 million to 5 million soldiers, and

Knowledge check 19

Did Stalin plan to invade western Europe in 1941, as the Germans later claimed?

Great Patriotic War The name given by the Soviets to their war with Germany (1941–45). It was meant to inspire the Russians to fight for their 'motherland', whatever their feelings about communist ideology.

Operation Barbarossa The codename for the German invasion of the USSR in June 1941.

there were significant changes in leadership and organisation to strengthen Soviet security. Stalin, however, reacted fiercely to the warnings from intelligence reports of Hitler's intentions to invade the USSR in the summer of 1941. He dismissed them as propaganda designed by the British government led by Churchill to lure the USSR into war against Germany. Hence, despite many warnings to Stalin, the Red Army was caught off-guard by the German invasion of June 1941. Stalin was so shocked that he was literally speechless for a number of days afterwards.

Hitler's *Blitzkrieg* in the USSR was spectacularly successful at first. By early December 1941 the German Army was only 32 km from Moscow itself. Hitler was so confident that victory against Russia was 'in the bag' that after the Japanese bombed Pearl Harbor, Hawaii, he declared war on the USA. Stiff resistance by the Red Army had delayed the Germans so much, however, that they failed to win the war before the Russian winter set in. A series of Soviet counterattacks at the end of 1941 pushed the Germans back from Moscow and effectively ended Hitler's chances of winning the Second World War.

The Grand Alliance

The USA's entry into the Second World War in December 1941 brought the USSR, the USA and Britain together in a Grand Alliance. Ideological differences were set aside, at least in theory, while the focus was on destroying Nazi Germany.

Most of the Second World War in Europe was fought along the Eastern Front between the Red Army and the German Army and its allies. Stalin expected support from the western powers and wanted to see the Americans and British engage in major warfare against the Germans on a '**second front**' in western Europe to relieve pressure on the Soviets on the Eastern Front. Churchill gave the Soviets the distinct impression that this would happen in 1942. Stalin was not at all impressed when he discovered the British Army was sent to fight in the sands of North Africa instead of France. Western assurances of the opening up of a real 'second front' in France in 1943 came to nothing. It was not until D-Day, 6 June 1944, that American, British and Commonwealth soldiers landed in France and finally opened the 'second front' that Stalin believed he had been promised two years earlier.

To Stalin's mind, the western allies' delay in opening the 'second front' was the result of a deliberate decision to minimise the casualties suffered by their armies, at the expense of the Red Army. Stalin saw D-Day as the West's response to the Red Army's progress towards Berlin. This meant that Stalin's attitude towards his western allies was one of suspicion and resentment. The western governments pointed to their supplies of military materials to the Red Army as a sign of their good faith, but Stalin was not impressed, as those supplies amounted to only 5 per cent of what the Red Army deployed. Hence, the Grand Alliance was never very *cordiale*, and it was only opposition to Hitler that kept it together. Nonetheless, as long as the war with Hitler lasted Stalin took care to keep his antagonism towards the West relatively hidden.

Western governments, 1933–45

There was a significant divergence in the motives, responses and methods of the western governments towards the USSR in the period from 1933 to 1945. On the one hand, there was considerable continuity in the foreign policies of Britain and France towards the

---

Knowledge check 20

What evidence is there that Stalin distrusted Hitler's longer-term ambitions, despite the Nazi–Soviet pact?

Blitzkrieg The German military tactic of fighting a lightning war with highly mobile mechanised formations, with tanks and air support closely coordinated.

'**Second front**' Most of the Second World War in Europe was fought along the Eastern Front. The USSR wanted the USA and Britain to engage in major warfare against Germany on a 'second front' in western Europe.

Knowledge check 21

Why was Stalin not appreciative of the supplies given to the Red Army by the USA and Britain during the war?

Soviet Union, in that they continued to be motivated by their antagonism to communism and wished to contain Soviet influence on European affairs. Nazi Germany, on the other hand, was committed to destroying both the USSR and '**Judeo-Bolshevism**'. Hitler claimed that communism was a Jewish conspiracy, since Karl Marx was Jewish, as were several prominent Bolsheviks in Russia, including Trotsky, Kamenev and Zinoviev. Most of the leaders of the Bavarian Soviet of April–May 1919, where Hitler lived at the time, were Jewish. In Hitler's embittered mind, anti-communism and anti-Semitism were conjoined. Italian foreign policy towards the USSR drifted from being aligned initially with Britain and France, into synchronisation with Germany, most conspicuously during the Spanish Civil War (1936–39).

Britain and France had struggled with economic crisis and political instability from the time of the Great Depression. Both struggled too to maintain their extensive empires in the face of growing challenges from subject peoples. Britain and France remained hostile to the USSR, however there was no immediate threat to Europe from the USSR. In fact, with the rise of Hitler the French saw Germany rather than the USSR as the greatest threat to peace. Hence the French agreed to allow the USSR to join the League of Nations in 1934. In 1935 France signed a defensive pact with the Soviet Union, though they refused to be drawn into making definite military guarantees to the USSR.

Britain too was prepared to accept the Soviet Union as a member of the League of Nations, but avoided making any military commitment to the Soviets. A key problem for the western governments was that Stalin's 'Terror' made him seem much more menacing than Hitler, as Hitler's regime was based to an overwhelming degree on popular consent. While Hitler presented German ambitions as being '**revisionist**' in nature, Marxists still looked for 'World Revolution'. In addition, the western governments were faced with the dilemma that any military intervention by the USSR against Germany would undermine Poland's sovereignty, and could have the effect of facilitating the extension of communism into the heart of Europe. Therefore, even in the summer of 1939, the western governments would not form a military alliance with Stalin, despite the probability of war with Germany.

Hitler's determination to destroy the USSR and its communist ideology was clear to everyone, though he was careful until August 1939 not to embroil Germany in a general European war prematurely. The Nazi–Soviet Pact failed to achieve Hitler's immediate aim of keeping Britain and France out of the war while he invaded Poland. The pact did serve to facilitate the German conquest of France in the summer of 1940, however, before Hitler turned his attentions against the Soviet Union in the following year.

The Grand Alliance

The British were extremely relieved to see the USSR enter the Second World War in June 1941. The entry of the USA into the war in December of that year made Germany's eventual defeat probable. In the meantime, the British fought the Germans and Italians in the marginal theatre of war in North Africa, and then in southern Italy, while promising Stalin that a significant 'second front' would be opened up in France in the not-too-distant future (see page 30). In fact, Stalin had to wait until D-Day in 1944 for the much-promised American–British troop landings in France. Stalin may

'**Judeo-Bolshevism**' Hitler used this term since he claimed that communism was a Jewish conspiracy.

'**Revisionist**' Hitler claimed that his foreign policies were 'revisionist' in the sense that he wanted to revise or correct some of the terms of the Treaty of Versailles (1919).

Knowledge check 22

Why would Poland not accept help from the Red Army against Germany?

well have been correct in suspecting that US president Franklin D. Roosevelt and Churchill were keen to minimise the number of casualties suffered by their armies, at the Russians' expense.

There is no question that during the war the overriding priority for the western allies was the defeat of Nazi Germany. At the same time they desired a postwar settlement that would ensure future peace, and were anxious to secure Soviet support for such a settlement. Churchill was anxious too for the Americans to invade Germany to prevent the Red Army sweeping all across Europe.

The impact of the Second World War on the USSR

The USSR suffered appallingly in the course of the war with Germany, with 27 million Soviet people killed and millions more left disabled. For comparison, the USA suffered 417,000 deaths in the war. The Soviet government calculated that up to $20 billion of damage was inflicted on the USSR by the Germans. Despite the several stunning victories over the Germans on the battlefield, the incredible human and economic losses suffered by the USSR meant that Soviet security was not assured for the future. Economically it was far weaker than the leading capitalist state in the postwar world, the USA, which came through the war virtually unscathed physically. Hence Stalin recognised that there could be advantages to working with the western governments to bring stability to Europe after the war, to neutralise any threat from Germany in particular, and perhaps even to secure American credits for the herculean task of rebuilding the Soviet Union once the war was over.

For Stalin, the future security of the Soviet Union was paramount. He believed that Soviet security would be enhanced by extending Soviet power deep into Europe, to create a buffer zone that would be under Moscow's control to insulate the USSR from future western threats. Stalin believed too that the Soviets' sacrifices during the war entitled them to compensation at the expense of Germany and its allies that had invaded the USSR. Though he did not state so explicitly, it is probable that Stalin saw the presence of the Red Army in eastern Europe at the end of the war as an opportunity to spread communism across the continent. He expected, in line with Marxist ideology, that the German proletariat would be amenable to communism once the Nazi regime had been exterminated. Hence Soviet concerns for security, and ambitions to spread Soviet power and communism, coalesced in Soviet plans for postwar Europe.

The Yalta Conference

The 'Big Three' — the leaders of the Grand Alliance: Stalin, US President Roosevelt and British prime minister Churchill — met at Yalta, in Crimea in the south of the USSR, in February 1945 to discuss what the future of Europe would be like once Hitler was defeated. In his dealings with Roosevelt and Churchill, Stalin emphasised the Soviets' security concerns and entitlement to compensation, and played down his ambitions to extend Soviet power eastwards in Europe. He was keen to see the western allies attack the Germans with the upmost vigour in the west, while the Red Army pummelled the Germans and their allies from the east. By the time of the Yalta Conference Marshal Zhukov's forces were only 65 km from Berlin itself.

Exam tip

Be sure to highlight how the tensions between the Soviets and their western allies in the Grand Alliance help to explain how the alliance fell apart so soon after the war, despite a desire on both sides to maintain it for a time.

Knowledge check 23

What did Stalin hope to gain through cooperation with the West after the war?

Stalin gave Roosevelt the impression that he was amenable to accepting the USA's vision for postwar Europe. He confirmed his agreement to the partition of Germany by the USSR, USA, Britain and France, and agreed to leave the more thorny questions about the ultimate future of Germany, and the reparations it would have to pay, for a future conference. He agreed that the USSR would join the **United Nations** at Roosevelt's request. He granted Roosevelt's wish for the conference to issue the Declaration on Liberated Europe, with its promises to allow the people of Europe to 'create democratic institutions of their own choice' and to establish governments after 'free elections'. Stalin also agreed to Roosevelt's request to join the USA and Britain in the war against Japan, three months after the war ended in Europe. In return, Roosevelt and Churchill acquiesced to Stalin's intention to retain the part of Poland that he had occupied following the Nazi–Soviet Pact, after he promised to compensate the Poles with German territory. All in all, Roosevelt was pleased with the conference and wrote to his wife that it had ended, 'successfully, I think'.

Stalin, however, claimed Roosevelt had understood that the Declaration on Liberated Europe was window-dressing: Stalin would allow elections to be held in the countries outside the USSR that were liberated by the Red Army, and he would not absorb them into the USSR as he had done with the Baltic states and Moldova (formerly Bessarabia), but he intended that each of them would be administered by governments that were 'friendly' towards the USSR. As a concession to the Americans, in the hope of maintaining East–West cooperation after the war, Stalin was willing to tolerate the establishment of coalition governments across eastern Europe, albeit with communists holding a very disproportionate share of the real power.

The Potsdam Conference

The Potsdam Conference held in July 1945 was a very different affair to that at Yalta. Its significance lies more in the relationship between Stalin and the new American president, Harry Truman, than in the agreements reached. The Americans finally accepted the Soviet plan to make the Oder–Neisse river form the new border between Germany and Poland, which was effectively a matter of accepting a fait accompli. Agreement was reached about German reparations to the USSR. Stalin reiterated his promise of 'free' elections in Poland, though the western leaders had no confidence that Stalin was in earnest. Otherwise, the most difficult questions, about the longer-term future of Germany and the question of peace treaties with Germany's former allies, were referred to future meetings of the victors.

The mood between Stalin and the western leaders verged on hostility. Stalin projected an image of strength and confidence. With Nazi Germany in ruins and the Red Army in place across Europe east of a line from Stettin on the Baltic to Trieste on the Adriatic, Stalin was in an extremely strong position to shape the fate of eastern Europe. Truman, for his part, was no less anxious to project American strength, and did so by confronting Stalin in very direct terms for failing to fulfil to the letter the Declaration on Liberated Europe. The news of the successful detonation of the USA's first atomic bomb gave Truman extra confidence in challenging Stalin, but the latter already knew about the 'Manhattan Project' and he did not react when Truman told him that the USA had developed a very powerful new weapon. The Potsdam Conference did not mark the start of the Cold War, as

United Nations An intergovernmental organisation that succeeded the League of Nations, and intended to be more effective in guaranteeing world peace in the future than its predecessor had been.

Knowledge check 24

What made Stalin think that he fulfilled his promises to the late President Roosevelt in the Declaration on Liberated Europe?

Exam tip

For any question in which you have to assign responsibility or blame for the Cold War, you must consider how both sides contributed to the postwar tensions in Europe.

both sides were anxious to avoid open conflict — but it signalled that the Grand Alliance was coming to an end.

Conclusions

The meeting of the American and Soviet armies at the Elbe in central Germany meant the end of Hitler's Reich but, as Churchill had feared, left Stalin effectively as the arbiter of the eastern half of Europe. To that extent, the aims of the western governments between 1933 and 1945 to contain Soviet power, and Hitler's aims to destroy it entirely, ended in complete failure. In the Yalta and Potsdam conferences the western allies achieved little real progress in reversing the territorial and political gains the Soviets had won on the battlefields.

Stalin was, by some key criteria, far more successful than the western governments in achieving his foreign policy aims. Thanks to his 'Second Revolution', and the economic, military and political transformation of the Soviet Union that it entailed, the USSR had not only survived the ferocious German onslaught but had emerged victorious at the end of the Second World War. The borders of the USSR had been extended westwards, and a series of satellite states was being established beyond those borders across eastern Europe.

Stalin claimed that Soviet foreign policy was focused primarily on the security of the USSR, but in fact there was always an underlying ambition to extend Soviet power and communist ideology if it was safe to do so. That dual emphasis on security and expansion was a consistent theme in Soviet foreign policy. As it happened, while the extension of the 'red empire' into eastern Europe undoubtedly strengthened Soviet security in some ways, it also posed challenges for the Soviet system in terms of imposing Moscow's control and communist ideology on people who resented both. Furthermore, despite all the achievements of the USSR in the war, Stalin's sense of insecurity, which was a key motive underlying his foreign policy, never disappeared.

Summary

- Stalin was the first world leader to fully appreciate the threat posed by Hitler's Nazi regime. His foreign policy after 1934 was focused on the aim of achieving 'collective security' against the German threat.
- Soviet attempts to achieve 'collective security' failed as a result of western governments regarding the USSR, particularly in view of Stalin's 'Terror', as a greater threat than Germany. This was especially so as Hitler reassured people that his foreign policy aims were no more than 'revisionist'.
- The Nazi–Soviet Pact reflected the Soviets' desperation to avoid being caught up in a general war while they were still vulnerable. Yet Stalin took advantage of the pact to enhance the security of the USSR and to spread communism.

- The German invasion of the USSR in June 1941 came very close to succeeding, but Stalin's leadership and the foundations laid down during the 'Second Revolution' allowed the Soviets to survive the invasion, and then to push the Germans out of the USSR.
- The Grand Alliance saw the USSR, USA and UK allied against Nazi Germany, but Stalin believed that the western allies left the Red Army to do the bulk of the fighting, and dying, in the war in order to minimise their own casualties. That meant relations between Stalin and his allies, even during the war, were far from positive.
- The USSR emerged from the Great Patriotic War as a victor, and its Red Army held sway over half of Europe. The involvement of the USA in European affairs, however, presented a new ideological challenge for the Soviets.

■ The search for security 1945–56

Stalin's foreign policy, 1945–56

Stalin's postwar motives were outlined in a speech he delivered in the Bolshoi Theatre in Moscow in February 1946. He was motivated, as ever, by Marxist–Leninist ideology. He reminded his audience of the inevitability of further conflict between communism and capitalism, with communism's victory being assured. Stalin's ideological aspirations were tempered with pragmatism, however. Because of the enormous toll exacted on the USSR during the course of the Great Patriotic War — 27 million deaths, millions of other casualties and the incredible destruction wrought on the west of the Soviet Union by Germany and her allies — Stalin realised that his foreign policy had to be cautious. Economically the USSR was far, far weaker than the USA and economic weakness had major implications for Soviet security.

The USSR needed time to rebuild after the war; the Five Year Plan of 1945 was designed to restore the Soviet economy to its pre-war strength. This suggests Stalin's postwar foreign policy was not primarily expansionist, as **Orthodox historians** used to argue. Orthodox historians were the first generation of American postwar historians who studied the Cold War, and theirs was the official American interpretation of the start of the Cold War until the 1960s saw a new generation of **Revisionist historians**. Revisionist historians argued that Stalin's postwar foreign policy was defensive. Nonetheless, most contemporary historians, generally associated with the Post-Revisionist school, would argue that Stalin's postwar foreign policy was motivated by a desire to spread Soviet power and communism as far as was possible without causing a war with the USA.

As early as October 1941 Stalin had informed the British Foreign Secretary, Anthony Eden, that he intended to keep the territories that had been annexed by the Soviet Union since the Nazi–Soviet Pact (August 1939). To placate American and British objections to the Soviet annexation of eastern Poland, Stalin offered to transfer to Poland the German territories east of the Oder–Neisse rivers, from which the German population had already fled ahead of the Red Army. Stalin was adamant that the borders of the USSR would be restored to where they stood in June 1941 and to where, with the exception of Finland, they stood in the time of Tsar Nicholas II. Roosevelt and Churchill had no choice but to accept Stalin's offer; they were in no position to alter the military facts on the ground in eastern Europe.

Stalin aimed to exercise 'influence' over eastern Europe beyond the borders of the USSR. This was understood by Churchill, who agreed to a rough demarcation of Soviet and British spheres of influence in eastern Europe with Stalin in October 1944. Roosevelt, however, rejected any such spheres in eastern Europe. Nonetheless, with the Red Army in place across eastern Europe, Stalin was effectively the master of half of Europe when the war in Europe came to an end in May 1945.

Stalin aimed to maintain Soviet influence in the region after the war, along with several subsidiary aims. He aimed to enhance the security of the USSR with an extensive buffer zone. He aimed to exact reparations from Germany and from

> **Knowledge check 25**
>
> What convinced Stalin that conflict was inevitable between the communist and capitalist powers?

> **Orthodox historians**
> Claimed that the Soviet Union was inherently expansionist and supported President Harry Truman's policy of containment.

> **Revisionist historians**
> Presented a new or revised interpretation of the Cold War, in which both of the superpowers contributed to the post-war tensions.

Germany's former allies in eastern Europe that had joined in the invasion of the USSR: Slovakia, Hungary, Romania and Bulgaria. He aimed also, needless to say, to export communism, and his ambitions were not confined to those areas already occupied by the Red Army. Stalin, true to his Bolshevik ideology, expected a communist revolution would occur in Germany soon after the war. He hoped that the French and Italians, and the Greeks, might become communists. He hoped to overawe the Turks and the Iranians on the USSR's southern borders.

At the same time, Stalin was anxious to maintain some level of cooperation with the West, and with the USA in particular. This was in order to guarantee the stability of the postwar peace settlement, as everyone was conscious of the fact that the Paris peace settlement of 1919 had unravelled completely within two decades of the First World War. Stalin also hoped to secure American loans and investment for reconstruction within the USSR that Roosevelt had led him to expect once the Second World War was over.

Historians' debate about the origins of the Cold War

Western historians have debated Stalin's motives, offering different suggestions as to whether his aims were mostly expansionist or mostly defensive. Influenced by George Kennan, Orthodox historians argued during the first decades of the Cold War that Soviet foreign policy was inherently expansionist. This means they believed the USSR was driven by ideology, and by its perceived security needs, to try to expand whenever possible. Revisionist historians, writing during or soon after the Vietnam War, were inclined to interpret Stalin's foreign policy aims as being primarily defensive, which seemed justified due to what Soviet citizens had suffered during the Second World War. They made the point that the Soviet Union was in no position to go to war against the USA, even without the atomic bomb being added to the equation. Revisionists argued that Stalin reacted to American threats — those of Truman's **'atomic diplomacy'**, the 'Truman Doctrine' (see page 39) and 'Marshall Aid' (see page 40). They interpreted Stalin's responses — tightening control over eastern Europe through Cominform (1947) and the Berlin Blockade (1948/9) — as reflections of Soviet insecurity.

Most contemporary historians criticise the Orthodox and Revisionist schools of historians for giving 'disproportionate attention' to either the role of expansionist ambitions or security concerns in the Soviet Union's postwar foreign policy. They argue that Stalin's immediate postwar goals focused mainly on security — but Stalin also expected Europe to become communist, as Lenin had done after the First World War. In 1946 Stalin said that he expected the Germans would soon embrace communism and the rest of Europe would follow. That ideological expectation, together with his desire for cooperation with the West to maintain the postwar settlement and his concern about the American atomic bomb, encouraged Stalin to be flexible in his foreign policy in the immediate postwar period.

Stalin's immediate postwar ambitions were to wield eastern Europe into a 'protective zone' for the USSR, and he planned to take reparations from Hitler's former allies in the region to help economic reconstruction in the Soviet Union. He was prepared to be flexible and sign the Declaration on Liberated Europe in order to maintain the Grand Alliance after the war. Stalin decided not to impose a Soviet system on eastern Europe straight away. His intention was to make eastern Europe communist in stages.

'Atomic diplomacy'
Refers to the Americans' use of the implied threat of nuclear warfare to curb Soviet ambitions.

Exam tip

This unit no longer requires you to master historiography. Nonetheless, an awareness of the lines of arguments of the main schools of historians about the origins of the Cold War will help you address questions on this unit.

Hence elections were held after the war and coalition governments that included communists were established. Soviet influence, however, ultimately depended on the Red Army and coercion. Stalin's increasingly dictatorial control over eastern Europe was seen by President Truman as a negation of the Declaration on Liberated Europe, and the Grand Alliance began to disintegrate once the war was over.

At the Potsdam Conference in July 1945 Stalin presented an image of Soviet strength, to make clear to the Americans that the USSR was strong enough to defend itself. He reacted with deliberate calm to President Truman's news about the development of an American atomic bomb, in order to disguise the Soviets' actual anxieties about the new weapon. Stalin's nonchalance was convincing because he had already known about the 'Manhattan Project' through espionage. He made it clear, without stating so explicitly, that he intended to retain a dominant position in eastern Europe. For example, he dismissed Churchill's complaints about the restrictions imposed on British diplomats in Bulgaria as 'fairy tales'.

Despite frosty relations, the Soviets and the western allies agreed to a series of treaties to conclude the war in eastern Europe. The Soviets, however, seemed keen to extend their influence beyond what Churchill called the 'Iron Curtain'. Not only did Stalin harbour ambitions about Germany, but he seemed indirectly to encourage the communists in Greece, put pressure on Turkey to allow the USSR to effectively control the Turkish Straits or Dardanelles, and he kept the Red Army in northern Iran after the date on which it was supposed to leave. In each case, Stalin hoped to extend Soviet influence without provoking a war, but his actions were interpreted in the West as proof of his desire for 'world domination'.

'Iron Curtain'
Churchill's term for the division of Europe by a virtually impenetrable barrier created by the Soviet Union.

Main events in Soviet foreign policy, 1945–56

The breakdown of the Grand Alliance

The Potsdam Conference (July 1945) effectively marked the end of the Grand Alliance. Nazi Germany, the main factor that kept the Alliance together, had been defeated. With Japan's surrender in August 1945 the Second World War had ended, but international relations were sliding towards an ideological Cold War. The new American president, Harry Truman, was more pugnacious in style than Roosevelt and more insistent that Stalin fulfil to the letter the promises he had made in the Declaration on Liberated Europe. Truman's personal hostility towards Stalin, however, and his use of what has been termed 'atomic diplomacy', simply antagonised Stalin without yielding any progress on the causes of conflict between the superpowers. Indeed, Stalin compared Truman with Hitler.

Knowledge check 26

Why was conflict between the superpowers highly probable after Germany's defeat?

From a Soviet perspective it was the Americans and British who destabilised the postwar truce between the two sides with their plans to rebuild the German economy. The Soviets had agreed to an American proposal during the war to de-industrialise as well as de-militarise and de-Nazify Germany. Stalin was keen for Germany to de-industrialise to guarantee Soviet security in the future. The British especially, and the Americans too, however, changed their minds in 1946 and decided that they could not afford to maintain a de-industrialised and hence dependent Germany. Furthermore, George Marshall, Truman's Secretary of State, devised a European Recovery Programme (ERP) to wean western Europeans away from communism by restoring western Europe to prosperity.

The Berlin Blockade

Rebuilding the economy in the three western sectors of Germany was seen as critically important for the rebuilding of the entire western European economy. Hence in April 1948 the Marshall Plan was put into effect, with $13 billion invested in western Europe over a number of years. As part of the plan a new German currency (the Deutschmark) was established and work started on investing Marshall Aid into the economy in western Germany. Stalin responded by having West Berlin blockaded from June 1948 in a bid to force the Allies out of the city or see the population of the western sectors starve. Nonetheless, he had no intention of finding the USSR in a third world war while the USA had the monopoly on the atomic bomb. Hence the Soviets were careful not to shoot down Allied planes during the airlift of food and fuel into West Berlin nor to do anything else that might trigger a war.

Once it was clear that the blockade would neither force the western Allies to stop rebuilding the economy of western Germany nor force them to leave West Berlin without a fight, Stalin called it off in May 1949. He was aware that the USA had stationed a number of B52 bombers, the type of plane that dropped atomic bombs on Japan in 1945, in bases in eastern England. As such, he decided not to risk the outbreak of war. The Soviets accepted the Berlin airlift as proof of American commitment to their policy of containment in Europe. Never again would the Soviets attempt to change the dividing lines between communism and capitalism in Europe through (even indirect) military means.

The end of the first Berlin crisis was soon followed by the formation of the Federal German Republic, or West Germany as it was popularly known. This was a democratic and capitalist satellite state of the USA. The Soviets responded in October 1949 with the establishment of the German Democratic Republic, popularly known as East Germany, a Soviet satellite with a population and economy that was only a fraction of that of West Germany.

The division of Germany into two ideologically opposed states was not what Stalin wanted. It meant that the 'Iron Curtain' looked set to divide communism and capitalism in Europe indefinitely.

One fact, however, reflects Stalin's overriding concern for security: in the '**Stalin Note**' of 1952 he offered to give up control over communist East Germany in return for a united but permanently disarmed Germany. It was a sincere offer to the West, but was rejected by the western governments because they distrusted the Soviets' intentions, though some West Germans later regretted the decision not to pursue the offer. Certainly, Stalin was no pacifist. There was a build-up of armies in the USSR's satellite states in south-eastern Europe in the early 1950s that seems to have been aimed at Yugoslavia, a communist state that acted independently of Moscow. Stalin's aggressive stance towards Yugoslavia reflected the fact that his foreign policy was never exclusively about security; the potential for Soviet aggression at a time when Stalin calculated that it would reap rewards was ever-present.

Western governments, 1945–56

Before the Second World War, the USA was not motivated by an ambition to spread its democratic and capitalist ideology beyond its borders. After the war, however,

'Stalin Note' An official proposal submitted by the Soviet Union for consideration by the West.

Exam tip

You will not have time in the examination to discuss in great detail what happened during the several events in this period, so you must concentrate on highlighting their significance for your answer.

it was. Like his predecessor, Franklin D. Roosevelt President Harry Truman was convinced that only democracy and capitalism could guarantee the stability of the world order and prevent the outbreak of another world war. The fact that the USSR was committed to spreading communist ideology, both in Europe and elsewhere, was seen by western governments as posing a real threat for the future.

The primary postwar aim of western governments was to achieve political stability. Roosevelt and Churchill had hoped to maintain the Grand Alliance for some time after the war in order to achieve that stability. Stalin, who was also keen to ensure the postwar peace settlement would endure, was at first willing to be flexible and cooperate with the West. Hence, Roosevelt persuaded Stalin to sign the Declaration on Liberated Europe. Stalin made it clear to Roosevelt and Churchill that he intended to exercise considerable 'influence' over eastern Europe. For domestic political reasons, however, the western leaders did not wish to define precisely how much 'influence' the Soviets intended to exercise.

In keeping with what he interpreted to be the unspoken understanding with Roosevelt, Stalin allowed elections to be held across eastern Europe after the war, and tolerated the formation of coalition governments — as long as local communist parties enjoyed significant shares of power in those governments, usually with control over the police and armies in the countries of eastern Europe. President Truman insisted that Stalin fulfil the Declaration on Liberated Europe to the letter, however — which simply antagonised the Soviets. The fact that the Americans monopolised control of postwar Japan made Stalin think that they were hypocritical in criticising him for doing the same in eastern Europe.

The Truman Doctrine

While Stalin was confident that conditions in western Europe in the immediate aftermath of the war would facilitate communist revolutions, the Americans were increasingly worried about that same possibility. A third of French and Italian voters were supporting communist candidates in elections. Communist insurgents looked likely to take control in Greece.

President Truman responded to Stalin's speech in the Bolshoi Theatre in February 1946, in which he predicted the inevitability of conflict between communism and capitalism, by asking George Kennan, a senior diplomat in the American embassy in Moscow, to explain what Stalin's intentions were. The result was Kennan's famous 'Long Telegram' of February 1946. Kennan identified what he considered the key motives underlying Soviet foreign policy after the Second World War. 'At bottom', he wrote, 'of [the] Kremlin's neurotic view of world affairs is traditional and instinctive Russian sense of insecurity.' He recommended that the USA pursue a long-term policy of patient but firm containment. One year later that policy was crystallised in the **Truman Doctrine**, the commitment made by the US government to contain the spread of communism, whether it was promoted by Soviet military power or by indigenous communist insurgents. Containment was the driving motivation in western foreign policy for the rest of the Cold War.

President Truman's announcement of the policy of containment in Congress in March 1947 was an immediate response to the communist insurgency in Greece and to Soviet pressure on Turkey to allow the USSR to take effective control of the Turkish

Truman Doctrine An important declaration of American foreign policy, committing the USA to containing the future spread of communism anywhere in the world.

Straits or Dardanelles. The policy had been under consideration for at least a year since it was recommended to Truman by Kennan, but the president was forced to act after the British government announced in February 1947 that it was no longer able to support the enemies of communism in Greece. Britain had been left bankrupt by the war, and was preoccupied with its impending withdrawal from India and Palestine. The USA, with its tremendous wealth and military power, had to take the leading role in implementing the policy of containment.

Marshall Aid

Truman's initial hope was that a public declaration of the USA's commitment to the policy of containment would suffice to restrain the Soviet Union's ambitions, especially given the USA's monopoly of the atomic bomb. Truman's new Secretary of State, George Marshall, however, returned to Washington after a tour of western Europe in the first part of 1947 convinced that far more was needed than a public declaration to save western Europe from succumbing to communism.

Knowledge check 27

How big a financial commitment was the ERP for the US government?

Marshall oversaw the drawing up of the European Recovery Programme (ERP), which he saw as vital for containing the spread of communism. Under the programme, popularly known as 'Marshall Aid', $13 billion was spent by the US government to revive the flagging economies of western Europe; this was equivalent to 10 per cent of the US federal government's budget over the period 1948–51. The programme was motivated primarily by the desire to wean western Europeans away from supporting communism by improving their living standards, by drawing them closer to the USA and by boosting their confidence to resist any pressures exerted by the Soviet Union. There was also a subsidiary motivation to undermine Soviet control over the states in eastern Europe by tempting them to seek financial support from the USA.

The rebuilding of the German economy, or at least that part of it within the three western sectors of Germany, was seen as vital for the success of the ERP. Hence the decision was taken in 1948 to establish a new German currency, the Deutschmark, and invest some 'Marshall Aid' to get the German economy restarted. Soviet objections were not allowed to reverse the decision once it was taken. American and British commitment to that decision was demonstrated with the Berlin Airlift in response to the Soviet blockade of West Berlin from June 1948. Truman, in particular, interpreted the blockade as a test of the USA's commitment to the policy of containment, and he showed the USA's determination not to appease Stalin. Following the appeasement of Hitler in the 1930s, the idea of appeasing Stalin was anathema to the western allies after the Second World War.

The ending of the Berlin Blockade in May 1949 was soon followed by the establishment of the Federal Republic of Germany (West Germany), which institutionalised the division of Germany for the remainder of the Cold War. West Germany enjoyed an 'economic miracle' in subsequent years and became a powerhouse for capitalism in western Europe. The West German government deliberately subsidised West Berlin to make it a showcase for capitalism right in the heart of communist East Germany.

'**Economic miracle**' The spectacular growth of the West German economy during the 1950s, by rates often of about 9 per cent per annum.

NATO

Another outcome of the Berlin crisis was the establishment of the Washington-led North Atlantic Treaty Organisation (NATO), a military alliance that committed the

USA to the use of military means to defend the status quo in western Europe against the possibility of Soviet aggression. The successful detonation of a Soviet atomic bomb in August 1949, followed by the success of the Chinese communist revolution in October 1949, undermined the Americans' confidence in their contest with the Soviet Union. After the outbreak of the Korean War in September 1950, NATO was transformed into a full-scale military alliance under American leadership. It marked the latest stage in the USA's escalating commitment to containing the spread of communism, through publicly made commitments, financial support for its anti-communist allies and finally full-scale military support.

The incorporation of West Germany into NATO in 1955 allowed the West to deploy German soldiers on the western side of the Iron Curtain, the front line of the Cold War in Europe. The Soviets responded by establishing the Moscow-led Warsaw Treaty Organisation, better known as the **Warsaw Pact**. It was a classic example of the 'security dilemma', where the actions of one side in a conflict to improve its security at the expense of the other inevitably prompt a retaliatory response to cancel out any hoped-for advantage.

Success?

It is difficult to assess the overall degree of success of the foreign policies of the USSR and the western governments between 1945 and 1956, because the best criteria by which to judge 'success' is questionable. A starting point would be to acknowledge Stalin's success in consolidating the Red Army's victory on the battlefield. Nazi Germany was utterly defeated by May 1945, mainly at the hands of the Red Army: 80 per cent of German casualties in the war were inflicted by the Soviets. Though the Soviets did not take it for granted that Germany would never cause another world war, the victory over Germany was so decisive that the Germans were never again in a position to threaten the security of the USSR.

Furthermore, the victories of the Red Army in the war left Stalin as the arbiter of the fate of the eastern half of Europe. He extended the borders of the USSR westwards by hundreds of miles. Beyond those borders Stalin established a buffer zone to enhance the security of the Soviet Union against any potential threat from the USA and its allies in western Europe. Over a number of years after the war Stalin steadily tightened his grip on the countries of eastern Europe, made their governments exclusively communist, subjected them to the Information Bureau of the Communist and Workers' Parties (**Cominform**) and controlled their economies through the Council for Mutual Economic Assistance (**Comecon**). The dissolution of Cominform by Stalin's successor, Khrushchev, in 1956 represented a loosening of Moscow's direct control over communist parties outside the USSR. Khrushchev brought the armies of the countries of eastern Europe directly under Moscow's control through the Warsaw Pact. In sum, the Soviets' postwar foreign policy may be considered successful in terms of enhancing the security of the USSR and extending Soviet influence and communist ideology well beyond its borders.

Nonetheless, there were disappointments too for the Soviets. The long-expected 'World Revolution' still did not materialise. Despite Stalin's objections, the Americans and British helped establish West Germany, with a population of 60 million, as a democratic and capitalist state that was very firmly in the western camp from 1949, and a member of the American-led NATO from 1955. The promising signs of

Warsaw Pact
A communist counterpart of the American-led NATO.

Exam tip

Since this unit requires discussion of the foreign policies of both the Soviet Union and the western governments, you must demonstrate how both sides contributed to the postwar tensions in Europe, even though you may decide that the Soviets were primarily to blame.

Cominform Established in October 1947 to coordinate the actions of communist governments and communist parties beyond the Iron Curtain and to keep them in line with Soviet policy.

Comecon Established to coordinate the economic development of the countries subject to Soviet control, Comecon was a Soviet response to the deep American involvement in the economies of western Europe.

growing support for communist parties in France and Italy in the aftermath of the war did not lead to revolutions in those countries either. Instead, American money, most spectacularly in the form of 'Marshall Aid', helped win the countries of western Europe to the USA's side in the Cold War.

After the failure of the Berlin Blockade in May 1949, the Soviet Union had to abandon any real hope of extending Soviet power beyond the Iron Curtain in the foreseeable future. Soviet foreign policy in Europe became overwhelmingly focused on defending what they already had. The Soviets could not compete with the USA in an arms race, mainly because of the disparity in the size of the economies of the superpowers. Hence Stalin offered the 'Stalin Note' in an attempt to de-escalate the Cold War. It was only after the death of Stalin, however, that relations between the superpowers began to 'thaw'.

As for the 'success' of the foreign policies of the western governments, there was both real achievement and real disappointments. The greatest disappointment was the unavoidable acceptance of Soviet domination across eastern Europe. Despite offering the 'carrot' of American money to help rebuild the USSR, and indulging in 'atomic diplomacy' as a 'stick' with which to threaten Stalin, the western governments had to accept, however reluctantly, that Soviet control to the east of the Iron Curtain could not be undone.

On the other hand, the foreign policy of the western governments was successful in their more modest aims of containing the spread of communism beyond the Iron Curtain. The United States found itself in a position of unrivalled leadership among western governments that were united by a fear of the Red Army and Stalin's ambitions. With strong support from the USA, western governments succeeded in restoring stability across western Europe after the war, and in establishing enduring democratic and capitalist societies that were tied to the USA ideologically, economically and militarily. The West German economy grew so spectacularly during the 1950s, by rates often of about 9 per cent per annum, that its growth was described as an 'economic miracle'. In fact, there was remarkable economic growth across the western half of mainland Europe in the early 1950s, which left Britain and Ireland lagging behind. As a result of this growth the western governments could feel that their system was better than communism — but the sense of insecurity persisted.

Summary

- There is a debate about Stalin's postwar foreign policy aims — about whether they were primarily expansionist or defensive, or what kind of combination they were of the two.
- Stalin's speech of February 1946 — coinciding as it did with the Soviet occupation of eastern Europe, a communist insurgency in Greece, and Soviet pressures exerted on Turkey and Iran — helped persuade President Truman to adopt a policy of containment to prevent the further spread of Soviet power or communism.
- Stalin's expectations that Germany and other countries in western Europe would soon become communist were disappointed. He then found himself reacting to American initiatives in western Europe, most notably the Marshall Plan and the rebuilding of the economy in western Germany that it entailed. Stalin's blockade of Berlin in 1948–49 served to underline the Americans' commitment to the policy of containment known as the Truman Doctrine.
- With the creation of the two German states in 1949, the division of Europe was fully institutionalised and took on the air of permanence.

Cooperation and coexistence 1956–79

Khrushchev's foreign policy, 1956–64

Khrushchev was, according to Robert Service, 'at once a Stalinist and an anti-Stalinist, a communist believer and a cynic, … a crusty philanthropist, a trouble-maker and a peacemaker … who was out of his intellectual depth'. His 'contradictory personality' was reflected in his Soviet foreign policy, wherein on the one hand he called for 'peaceful coexistence' at the Geneva Conference in July 1955. Later, however, he threatened the Americans by saying, 'History is on our side — we will bury you.' As a Marxist, Khrushchev was convinced that communism would eventually win out — and boasted that the USSR was making missiles 'like sausages'!

Khrushchev's foreign policy had several motives. On the one hand there was his fear that the alternative to 'peaceful coexistence' would be the most destructive war in history and, having been in charge at Stalingrad during the awful German assault on that city during the Great Patriotic War, he was haunted by the spectre of war. He was also motivated by a wish to divert resources from military spending into raising living standards. Stalin's Five Year Plans had been focused primarily on heavy industry and armaments. By the mid-1950s there was a prevailing feeling within the Soviet Union, and across eastern Europe, that the Bolshevik Revolution had yet to deliver the quality of life that Marxism promised. Khrushchev hoped to address that problem.

He acknowledged, 'Communist society cannot be built without an abundance of bread, meat, milk, butter and vegetables and other agricultural products.' His 'virgin lands' project was designed to deal with the basic struggle of the USSR to feed its own people comfortably. Yet Khrushchev was a sincere Bolshevik in that he took it for granted that Marxism–Leninism was inherently superior to capitalism and believed that 'World Revolution' was inevitable though, unlike Stalin, he was confident that it could be achieved by (mostly) peaceful means. He wanted 20 years of 'peaceful coexistence' to catch up economically with the USA and to prove that communism was the best economic system for society.

Khrushchev made major cuts to the Soviet Union's conventional armed forces and diverted resources into consumer goods. Yet billions of roubles were invested in rocket systems and nuclear weapons to enhance Soviet prestige and security — which meant that the promised improvement in living standards never fully materialised. Furthermore, Khrushchev was afraid to make major changes to the system he had inherited from Stalin. His economic reforms, for example, even in agriculture, were too limited to deal with Russia's continuing economic weaknesses.

Khrushchev was sincere in his wish to make Soviet society more free. He adopted a 'new course' compared with that of Stalin. He freed political prisoners from the infamous gulags and reined in the apparatus of state repression that had been built up under Lenin and especially under Stalin. He wanted to win the support of Soviet citizens for the Soviet system, and not depend so much on 'Terror' as Stalin had done.

'Peaceful coexistence' Instead of engaging in a Cold War, which carried the risks of becoming an actual war, the ideological rivals could each engage in peaceful competition on behalf of their own ideology.

Knowledge check 28

How was Khrushchev's military spending contradictory?

'New course' Promised to improve the quality of people's lives, in contrast to Stalin's emphasis on the state's authority and security.

His 'de-stalinisation' speech at the Communist Party of the Soviet Union's 20th Congress in February 1956, in which he called Stalin a 'monster and a tyrant' for the arrest, imprisonment and killing of huge numbers of innocent people, stunned his audience, but reflected his vision of a humane form of communist governance that he hoped to exercise not only in the Soviet Union but across the communist world.

Khrushchev, therefore, was well-intentioned. In foreign policy, however, his overriding concern was for the security of the USSR, and the maintenance of Soviet authority over eastern Europe. This was for security reasons but also for ideological reasons: he could not allow the progress of communism to seem reversible. Hence, despite major differences of emphasis compared with Stalin, there was a lot of continuity in Soviet foreign policy under Khrushchev.

Peaceful coexistence

After Stalin's death, the Politburo's immediate foreign policy priority was to de-escalate the Cold War. It recognised that not only had Stalin's aggressive style of foreign policy had the counterproductive effect of uniting the western European governments under the USA's leadership, it had also locked the USSR into an arms race with the Americans that the Soviet economy simply could not sustain. Hence the Politburo aimed to improve Soviet security by promoting the idea of peaceful coexistence between the world's two main ideological systems. The new Soviet leaders were very keen for a 'thaw' in East–West relations.

Khrushchev promoted the 'Spirit of Geneva' on meeting US President Dwight 'Ike' Eisenhower in 1955. This meeting of the American president and the Soviet premier at Geneva was the first such conference since Potsdam in 1945. The two sides came to an agreement on the future of Austria. Khrushchev's withdrawal of the Red Army from Austria in 1955 was intended as a striking gesture to underline the fact that he had no territorial ambitions in Europe. He made it very clear that the establishment of the Warsaw Treaty Organisation (the Warsaw Pact) was a direct response to the Americans' decision to integrate West Germany into NATO in 1955, and the Warsaw Treaty explicitly stated that it would be dissolved when NATO was dissolved. The security of the 'Soviet empire' was his top priority, as it had been for Stalin.

Eastern Europe

In relation to the USSR's satellite states in eastern Europe, Khrushchev was willing to show some degree of flexibility in allowing governments to 'tweak' the Soviet system as it operated in their states — but there was no question of allowing them to shape their own destinies. He saw eastern Europe as vital for Soviet security, and for the future of communism. The move away from Stalinist Terror, however, made protest seem possible in the Soviet satellite states. The Red Army had to intervene to quell anti-Soviet protests in East Germany in 1953. After Khrushchev's 'de-stalinisation' speech there were hopes for real change in eastern Europe. On top of the general resentment at the imposition of Soviet control and communism by the Red Army after the Second World War, there was growing dissatisfaction about living standards. These remained disappointingly poor, especially when compared with those in western Europe where an 'economic miracle' was transforming lives for the better.

'De-stalinisation' speech Khrushchev denounced Stalin's cult of personality and condemned his 'excesses'.

Knowledge check 29

How was Khrushchev's foreign policy more consistent with that of Stalin than his stated intentions had led many contemporaries to expect?

'Spirit of Geneva' The positive atmosphere generated by the meeting of the American president and the Soviet premier at Geneva in 1955.

In Poland there were wide disturbances in the summer of 1956, in which at least 50 people were killed. That crisis was averted when Khrushchev accepted the election of Władysław Gomułka as head of a reformist communist government in Poland in October 1956, as long as there were no changes to Soviet–Polish relations. Khrushchev recognised that economic problems undermined any hope of winning the people's commitment to communism, and he accepted that there were 'different paths to socialism'.

Hungary presented a graver problem. In 1956 Khrushchev promoted the reformist Communist Imre Nagy to take charge of Hungary, in the expectation that he would resolve the unrest in that Soviet satellite. Nagy, however, became swept up by the general mood in Hungary to emulate the Austrians, whose country had the previous year been formally acknowledged as democratic and neutral. Because the Austrians and Hungarians had jointly controlled the Austro-Hungarian empire until the end of the First World War, many Hungarians envied the Austrians their new-found freedoms.

Nagy's decision to call democratic elections in Hungary, which the communists would inevitably lose and which would pull Hungary out of the Warsaw Pact, was therefore seen as a direct threat to Soviet control over eastern Europe and hence a threat to Soviet security. This would also have represented a major ideological setback for the communist world. Khrushchev, under pressure from other members of the Politburo and the Soviet military, felt he had no option but to use the Red Army to crush the 'Hungarian Uprising' in November 1956. Nagy was executed as a warning to other leaders in eastern Europe not to challenge Soviet control. His place was taken by János Kádár, a man who was unquestionably loyal to Moscow, though also willing to experiment with economic reforms that in time resulted in Hungarians enjoying some of the best living standards in eastern Europe, though still far lower standards than those enjoyed in the West.

The 'economic miracle' enjoyed by West Germany since the Marshall Plan restarted its economy in 1948–49 posed another problem for Khrushchev, in that it threatened to undermine the very existence of East Germany (the GDR). The much higher incomes, and much greater freedoms, enjoyed in West Germany caused more than 2 million people to leave East Germany for the West after 1949: 190,000 left East Germany in 1960 alone. Those who left tended to be well-educated, skilled and young, and their disappearance damaged and discredited the regime of the East German leader, Erich Honecker, and communism itself. After a series of embarrassingly futile negotiations with the USA from 1958, Khrushchev eventually sanctioned the building of the Berlin Wall in August 1961. The wall quickly became an embarrassing symbol of the repressive nature of communism, but it served its purpose very effectively. It saved communist East Germany for almost another three decades, resolved the Berlin problem (of how to close the gap in the Iron Curtain that was West Berlin) and brought stability to Europe.

Contradictions

Rather than risk conflict in Europe, Khrushchev focused his ideological ambitions on the developing world. He spent billions to spread Soviet influence and communism outside Europe in mostly peaceful competition with the USA. Khrushchev's dual strategy in search of security and ideological expansion shows consistency with other Soviet leaders. The contradictions between Khrushchev's ostensibly peaceful intentions

Knowledge check 30

Why did Khrushchev believe that he had no choice but to crush the 'Hungarian Uprising'?

Knowledge check 31

Why were Khrushchev's attempts to negotiate a solution about West Berlin with Washington unsuccessful?

and his use of passionate anti-imperialist rhetoric — most famously at the United Nations in October 1960 when he struck the podium with his shoe for emphasis — not to mention his readiness to use force, as in Hungary, resulted in a foreign policy that seemed contradictory and inconsistent. Khrushchev's critics within the USSR, and in China, condemned him for unwisely trying to intimidate the new American president, John F. Kennedy, before being forced into humiliating climbdowns, as happened with Berlin (1958–61) and again with the **Cuban Missile Crisis** (1962). Foreign policy failures, and his failure to deliver the economic progress that he promised, sealed his fate and he was persuaded to retire as Soviet leader in October 1964.

Western governments, 1956–64

Ike Eisenhower became the president of the USA in 1953. He was a former general, elected as a **Cold Warrior** who promised to '**roll back**' communism. One of his loudest supporters was the notorious Senator Joseph McCarthy. Eisenhower was never likely to trust the Soviets sufficiently to grasp any opportunity that there may have been to end the Cold War in the immediate aftermath of Stalin's death. This was despite Churchill's encouragement to consider the possibility that the post-Stalin Politburo might be sincere. On the other hand, Eisenhower proved to be more pragmatic in practice than his anti-communist rhetoric had led many to expect. His top priority after his election was the security of the USA and the containment of communism, not just in Europe but around the world. American security and the containment of communism were seen to be inseparable. Nonetheless, he was keen to avoid war with the Soviet Union, or even a proxy war such as the one just ending in Korea.

> **Exam tip**
>
> Because this unit considers both sides in the Cold War equally, you should highlight Eisenhower's contribution to maintaining Cold War tensions despite the Soviet desire for 'peaceful coexistence' in the mid-1950s.

In order to guarantee the security of the West, Eisenhower sanctioned a massive programme of nuclear armament. American nuclear weapons were meant to counterbalance the large size of the Red Army, providing 'deterrence on the cheap'. They were the central feature of the policy of Mutually Assured Destruction (MAD). Eisenhower and his advisers expected that any war between the superpowers would inevitably escalate into a nuclear confrontation in which both the USA and the USSR would suffer catastrophic damage. They wanted to ensure that the cost of any war between the superpowers would be so great that neither side could allow it to happen. By 1960 the USA possessed 40,000 nuclear weapons, far more than the USSR. The Soviets led in the Space Race, however, having successfully launched the first man-made satellite, Sputnik, into space in October 1957 and put the first man into space, Yuri Gagarin, in April 1961. The Soviet investment in space was intended to boost the prestige of Khrushchev, the USSR and communism. It had the unintended effect, however, of making the Americans anxious lest the Soviets weaponise space.

Where Europe was concerned, Eisenhower was confident about maintaining the status quo. Western Europe was entirely dependent on the USA, through NATO, to

> **Exam tip**
>
> Students sometimes get confused about the disparity between Khrushchev's intentions and his actions. Make sure that you can account for them clearly.

Cuban Missile Crisis Caused by the deployment in 1962 of Soviet nuclear missiles in Cuba, a country only 90 miles off the coast of the USA. President John F. Kennedy successfully insisted that the missiles be withdrawn.

Cold Warrior An American who claimed to be zealously opposed to communism.

'**Roll-back**' Eisenhower had criticised President Truman for simply containing communism. He promised to 'roll back' (get rid of) communism in places where it had been established.

> **Knowledge check 32**
>
> Why was the Space Race such a prominent part of the Cold War?

guarantee its security against any possible Soviet aggression. The USA's predominance in the West was also based on its overwhelming economic strength, and its active support for the growth of the economies of western Europe as a defence against the lures of communist ideology. American culture, particularly its movies, popular music, fashion and enviable lifestyles, cemented western Europeans' enthralment to the USA.

The greatest problem for Eisenhower in his relations with western Europe was the management of the process of **decolonisation**. The 1950s and 1960s saw the dismantling of the European empires, as a result of growing demands for independence together with economic problems at home. Yet the British and French governments, in particular, hoped to hold on to some of the more valuable parts of their empires. The Americans were inherently hostile to the concept of empires, and encouraged decolonisation despite some concern in case the newly independent former colonies might be tempted into the communist camp. Hence, when Britain and France joined with Israel in October/November 1956 in a crude attempt to assert their power over the valuable Suez Canal in Egypt, President Eisenhower was infuriated, especially as that adventurism coincided with the Hungarian Uprising. The president used the USA's power, both economic and diplomatic, to quickly end the Suez Crisis by forcing the British, French and Israelis to withdraw. The episode served as a stark reminder to the European powers of their dependence on Washington.

As for Hungary, Eisenhower never had any intention of getting directly involved in affairs on the Soviet side of the Iron Curtain. Despite his early rhetoric about 'roll-back,' he wanted stability in Europe, not open conflict. In that modest goal he largely succeeded. After the tumultuous changes across Europe in the aftermath of the Second World War and the uncertainty that characterised the years that followed, most dramatically during the Berlin Blockade, President Eisenhower's term of office felt reassuringly calm. The two superpowers seemed to have reached a modus vivendi, especially where Europe was concerned.

John F. Kennedy was elected as the president of the USA in 1960 after campaigning strongly as a Cold Warrior and criticising Eisenhower for settling for stability rather than pursuing victory in the Cold War. Nonetheless, once he was inaugurated as president, Kennedy showed himself to be level headed. He was criticised by Willy Brandt, the mayor of West Berlin, for not responding strongly to the building of the Berlin Wall in August 1961. It is difficult to see what Kennedy could have achieved through threats of aggression, however, and he recognised that the resolution of the Berlin crisis in 1961 helped maintain peace in Europe. He commented philosophically, 'It's not a very nice solution but a wall is a hell of a lot better than a war.' He satisfied himself by exploiting the Berlin Wall for anti-communist propaganda with his famous 'Ich bin ein Berliner' speech of June 1963. He was assassinated in Dallas, Texas, in November of that year.

Overall, in terms of success, one can point to the stabilisation of the Cold War in Europe during the terms of office of presidents Eisenhower and Kennedy. Both promised more while campaigning for the presidency than they delivered in office. That, however, was simply because as the president of the USA they had to acknowledge that any American attempt to challenge the Soviet Union on the eastern side of the Iron Curtain could have provoked the outbreak of a nuclear war.

Decolonisation The process by which the remaining European empires, chiefly those of Britain and France, were dismantled and new states formed across southern Asia and Africa.

Exam tip

Don't spend much time in an examination discussing decolonisation. A quick reference to it as a source of tension between the USA and its most important allies in western Europe is likely to be all that is required.

Knowledge check 33

Why did candidates for the American presidency invariably present themselves as fierce anti-communists?

To keep their western allies united under the USA's leadership, and to ensure that communism did not threaten to take control of any country west of the Iron Curtain, was no mean feat. In fact, the difficulties experienced by the Soviets in keeping control over the countries of eastern Europe, and the fact that the Soviets were obliged to sanction the building of the Berlin Wall, indicated that the West was winning the Cold War in Europe. The Soviet reaction to the Hungarian Uprising in 1956 underlined, for the world to see, that the 'red empire' was maintained chiefly by the threat of military force. Not only was it a propaganda disaster for the prestige of the Soviet Union, it alienated many of the people in western Europe who had been sympathetic to Marxist ideology until that point. It also proved to be a setback for Sino–Soviet relations. Hence, it can be concluded that where Europe was concerned, the years 1956 to 1964 were much more successful from a western viewpoint than they were for the Soviet Union.

Brezhnev's foreign policy, 1964–79

Leonid Brezhnev became the leader of the USSR in October 1964. Like that of his predecessor, Khrushchev, Brezhnev's foreign policy for Europe was motivated more by ensuring the security of the Soviet system than by spreading communism. Learning from Khrushchev's blunders, Brezhnev adopted a cautious foreign policy. He avoided direct confrontations with the West. He aimed to build Soviet military strength so that the USA would be obliged to treat the USSR as an equal on the world stage. Hence under Brezhnev the Soviet Union invested heavily in building up its conventional forces while also striving towards parity with the USA in terms of nuclear weapons capability. As the Soviets' military strength grew, however, Brezhnev consciously aimed to project Soviet power and to promote communism on a global scale. In that he was largely successful, not solely because of the strengths of the USSR but also because much of his term of office coincided with a prolonged period of American self-doubt and angst about its economic decline and foreign policy failures.

Main events in Soviet foreign policy, 1964–79

Czechoslovakia

Under Brezhnev's premiership the USSR enjoyed steady if modest economic growth, of between 2.5 to 3 per cent per annum. Growing exports of oil allowed him to improve living standards while also engaging in significant increases in military spending. Subsidised sales of oil to its satellites helped to hold the 'red empire' together, with economic incentives supplementing the threat posed by the Red Army. The Soviet system, however, still could not match the West's wealth and productivity.

To Alexander Dubček, the new leader of Czechoslovakia in 1968, it was clear that deep economic and political reforms were needed to make communism work as well as capitalism was clearly working in the West. Brezhnev worried, however, that the radical nature of the 'Prague Spring' from January 1968 would undermine the practice of communism and weaken Moscow's control over its satellites. When he could not persuade Dubček to cancel his reforms, Brezhnev deployed the Warsaw Pact forces to crush the 'Prague Spring' in August 1968.

Knowledge check 34

Since the economies of the Soviet bloc states grew fairly steadily in the 1950s and 1960s, why were so many people in eastern Europe, including the Czechs, so dissatisfied?

The Brezhnev Doctrine

After crushing the 'Prague Spring' Brezhnev took the opportunity to announce the 'Brezhnev Doctrine' to make it clear to everyone, both the people under the control of a communist government and to the communists' enemies, that the USSR would not tolerate any threat to the control of any communist government, wherever it was established in the world. Brezhnev's reassertion of Soviet control over Czechoslovakia can be interpreted as a reflection of the Soviets' continuing sense of insecurity, but the Brezhnev Doctrine can also be seen as an indication of confidence. Brezhnev made significant efforts to spread communist ideology in the **Third World**, and cited the doctrine to justify the Soviet intervention in Afghanistan in 1979.

Détente

Unlike the negative impact of Khrushchev's actions against the Hungarians in 1956, Brezhnev's actions against the Czechs did not affect the superpowers' relations. Both sides were equally keen for **Détente** to reduce the risk of war. That policy was extremely popular with Europeans on either side of the Iron Curtain, and was seen as offering some hope that the barriers dividing them might one day be overcome.

Brezhnev was happy to allow Willy Brandt, West Germany's Chancellor from 1969, to pursue his policy of *Ostpolitik*, to gradually improve relations between the two Germanies and to ease tensions across the Iron Curtain generally. The Quadripartite Protocol (1971) and the Basic Agreement (1972) seemed to resolve the **German Question** in a way that was compatible with Soviet interests.

The Helsinki Accords (1975) were signed by all the countries of Europe, except Albania for a time. The signatory states acknowledged the postwar borders of Europe to be inviolable, and agreed to respect human rights and other fundamental freedoms and to cooperate with each other in economic, scientific and humanitarian endeavours. The Accords promised stability across Europe, and seemed to make the postwar settlement in Europe permanent. Meanwhile, the signing of the first Strategic Arms Limitations Treaty (SALT 1) in 1972 was seen by all sides as a significant step towards defusing the risk of a nuclear holocaust. Within Europe the era of Détente was welcomed by governments and people on both sides of the Iron Curtain as a time of progress towards the establishment of a Europe in which two very different ideological systems could peacefully coexist. There was optimism that the governments of eastern Europe would allow greater freedom and more civil rights to their citizens, albeit gradually, as East–West tensions subsided.

Yet, despite Détente, Brezhnev took advantage of US weakness in the 1970s to support the spread of communist ideology in Indo-China, around the Horn of Africa and in southern Africa, and in Nicaragua in Central America. Brezhnev's involvement in the Third World was primarily driven by ideological ambition, but it also reflected the Soviets' concerns about China's ambition to play the leading role in communism, as well as Brezhnev's desire to enhance his personal prestige and not just that of the USSR. With hindsight it is clear that the era of Détente, or the 'Brezhnev era' as it was commonly known, was the heyday of the Soviet Union.

Third World The term used in the Brezhnev era to signify countries that were not aligned with either the communist bloc or NATO.

Détente Signified the lessening of tensions between the superpowers, through greater dialogue, less hostile actions against their rivals, and negotiations about arms control.

Ostpolitik A new foreign policy devised by the West German government to try to improve relations between West Germany and its neighbours, chiefly East Germany but also the USSR and Poland.

German Question The challenge of satisfying German national aspirations while maintaining peace in Europe.

Knowledge check 35

In what sense was the heyday of the Soviet Union a mirage?

Western governments, 1964–79

A major reason why the Soviet Union seemed so strong in the Brezhnev era was that the USA was distracted by a series of problems. The nightmare of the war in Vietnam formed the backdrop to American foreign policy from 1965 onwards. American interest in Europe was diminished because the Iron Curtain gave every appearance of being permanent. President Lyndon Johnson surprised the Soviet ambassador to Washington by his nonchalant reaction to the Warsaw Pact's intervention in Czechoslovakia in August 1968. Johnson, and his successor Richard Nixon, were obsessed with searching for a way to get the USA out of the Vietnamese quagmire 'with honour'. The Americans hoped to secure Soviet and/or Chinese assistance in extricating themselves from Indo-China without admitting defeat at the hands of what Johnson called 'a raggedy-assed fourth-rate country'. That was a major motive for the Americans' support for Détente.

Economic difficulties in the 1970s gave the Americans additional incentives for Détente. The predominance that American manufacturers had enjoyed in the world markets since the end of the Second World War was increasingly being challenged by western European and Japanese competitors. Japanese products, which combined better quality with lower prices, were a particular challenge for American companies, which had grown complacent during the long absence of serious competition. In addition, the price of oil, which was critical for the US economy, rose very significantly as oil-producing countries insisted on fairer remuneration. Unemployment and inflation rose in the USA, and the US government was obliged to curtail some of its massive spending on defence and on its prestigious but very expensive space projects. The public and political mood in the USA turned against any more overseas 'adventures' after the Vietnam War, and Washington did not respond robustly to Soviet support for communists in Africa or even in Nicaragua.

The progress made by the USSR in the Cold War began to create unease among a growing number of Americans in the second half of the 1970s, however. One opinion poll revealed that 70 per cent of Americans believed the Soviets had taken advantage of Détente to strengthen their own position at the USA's expense. Jimmy Carter, who was elected as US president in 1976, had major concerns about the Soviets' global ambitions and was encouraged by his National Security Adviser, Zbigniew Brzezinski, to adopt a tough stance with the USSR. Carter insisted that the Soviets abide by the terms of the Helsinki agreement with regards to human rights, religious freedom and self-determination. He also significantly increased US military spending.

US foreign policy suffered two major setbacks under Jimmy Carter, however. In April 1978 a military coup in Afghanistan saw a communist regime established in that country. A revolution in neighbouring Iran in January and February 1979 toppled the Shah, one of the USA's chief allies in south-western Asia, and saw him replaced by a virulently anti-American Islamic government led by the Ayatollah Ruhollah Khomeini. When Brezhnev sent the Red Army into Afghanistan in December 1979 at the request of its communist government, Carter and Brzezinski interpreted this as a move by the Soviets to further threaten the USA's crucial supplies of oil from the Middle East, which were already disrupted by the Iranian Revolution. They were even

Knowledge check 36

Why was President Johnson so nonchalant about the 'Prague Spring' being crushed?

Knowledge check 37

How might Brzezinski's Polish background have influenced his advice to President Carter about dealing with the Soviet Union?

Knowledge check 38

Why were the Americans so troubled by the Red Army's intervention in Afghanistan?

concerned that Brezhnev planned to use the Red Army in Afghanistan to link up with the communist states in the Horn of Africa and dominate the entire region. Détente was dead.

Success?

The years after Stalin's death in 1953 saw the Cold War in Europe stabilise and the threat of war recede. The fact that both sides had nuclear weapons meant that war between them was inconceivable. Both sides were willing to acquiesce to 'peaceful coexistence' or Détente where Europe was concerned. Ideological ambitions were focused on the Third World, where a small number of proxy wars were fought without risking wider confrontations because the policy of MAD threatened to destroy mankind if conventional conflicts ever escalated into a nuclear war.

Arguably, it was Brezhnev's ideological ambitions in the 1970s to spread communism globally, and his continuation of the massive build-up of the Soviet Union's nuclear and conventional military strength despite the policy of Détente and the signing of SALT 1, that prompted a shift in American foreign policy in 1979. By that stage a majority of Americans believed that Détente had failed because the Soviets had taken advantage of it to strengthen themselves at the USA's expense. Ronald Reagan directed fierce rhetoric against President Jimmy Carter in the presidential election campaign of 1980. This was inspired not only by Carter's own failings but by what Reagan, and many Republicans, considered to be the failure of American foreign policy throughout the era of Détente. The Soviet intervention in Afghanistan in 1979 was the trigger, but not the cause, of what became the 'Second Cold War'.

Knowledge check 39

What killed Détente?

Summary

- After Stalin's death the Soviet Politburo was keen to see the Cold War replaced by 'peaceful coexistence', wherein the two superpowers could compete peacefully in support of their respective ideologies. The new American president, Eisenhower, was a 'Cold Warrior', however, and was deeply hostile to the Soviet bloc.
- Despite fierce Cold War rhetoric and massive investment in nuclear weapons, the two superpowers achieved a mutual understanding in Europe, and the division of Europe came to be seen as permanent. The Americans did not intervene in support of the people in eastern Europe who were unhappy about being subject to Soviet domination.
- The Brezhnev era was the heyday of the Soviet Union, with steady if unspectacular economic growth and a build-up of Soviet conventional and nuclear forces guaranteeing its security.
- Détente was very popular among Europeans on both sides of the Iron Curtain.
- The Soviet build-up of its nuclear weaponry, and its sponsorship of communist governments in many parts of the Third World, undermined most Americans' support for Détente, even before the Red Army's intervention in Afghanistan spelled its end.

■ Soviet aggression, decline and collapse 1979–91

Soviet foreign policy, 1979–91

Brezhnev sent the Red Army into Afghanistan in December 1979 to stabilise the communist regime that had taken power in Kabul the previous year. It was regarded by the Soviets as a defensive move, motivated by a desire to preserve a communist regime in difficulty, in keeping with the Brezhnev Doctrine. It was interpreted by US President Jimmy Carter as an aggressive act, however, and as a reflection of wider Soviet ambitions to dominate the Middle East, a part of the world seen as vital for American interests. All Americans regarded it as the end of Détente.

The Soviet leadership was taken by surprise by the strength of the American reaction to events in Afghanistan. Their former sense of insecurity returned with a vengeance, especially when Carter was replaced by Ronald Reagan as the American president in 1981. The USSR found itself locked into a 'Second Cold War' against a USA that was more self-confident and more openly antagonistic towards communism than it had been for decades. The aged Soviet leadership of the time, and a very great many Europeans, were anxious over much of the period that President Reagan would spark off a nuclear war — and this overwhelmingly motivated Soviet foreign policy from the end of 1979. The primary aim of the Soviet government through the first half of the 1980s was to protect the Soviet Union from what it perceived to be the very real possibility of an American attack. It also hoped to maintain the status quo across the Soviet empire as far as possible, but that turned out to be less important for the USSR than its own survival.

> **'Second Cold War'** A period of renewed tensions between the superpowers, from the Red Army's intervention in Afghanistan to when Mikhail Gorbachev began to ease tensions from 1985.

There was a growing recognition in the Politburo that the traditional methods of Soviet foreign policy were not sufficient for the new situation they found themselves in. The Soviet Union could not keep pace, either financially or technologically, with the new arms race launched by Reagan on becoming president. The Soviet leadership realised as early as 1980 that they could not risk provoking an American response by military intervention in eastern Europe if the Soviet satellite states were to rebel. Soviet foreign policy became a desperate search for security.

The Afghan war, the Second Cold War and the decline of the USSR, 1979–85

President Carter interpreted the Red Army's intervention in Afghanistan as a resumption of the Cold War. He responded by organising a boycott of the 1980 Olympic Games held in Moscow. More importantly, he imposed a trade embargo on the USSR, with the embargo on grain exports proving to be particularly punishing because it highlighted the failings of communist economics in a way that directly affected Soviet citizens — through the resultant shortage of food. There was no real hunger in the Soviet bloc caused by the blockade, but the demoralising queues for food sapped popular morale over time.

Western European governments were ambiguous about the end of Détente. This was reflected in the uneven support given to the American-led boycott of the Moscow

Olympic Games. The British government under prime minister Margaret Thatcher was very supportive of the USA's robust response to the Soviet intervention in Afghanistan, with Thatcher very keen to build a 'special relationship' with President Reagan. Other western European governments were reluctant to throw away all that had been achieved through Détente, especially the West German government under Chancellor Helmut Schmidt. Schmidt travelled to Moscow in 1980 to maintain a positive relationship with Moscow.

Nonetheless, despite the fact that they did not all agree with the end of Détente, the governments of western Europe were reluctant to defy the Americans. The Soviet deployment of highly mobile SS20 missiles in eastern Europe from the end of 1979 underlined the West's dependence on the USA, and on NATO in particular, for its security. Western European governments agreed to NATO's deployment of Pershing and cruise missiles to counter the new Soviet threat, despite massive public opposition to the new arms race. The new missile systems, and Reagan's bellicose rhetoric, convinced more than half of Europeans by 1983 that there would be an all-out war between the superpowers in their lifetimes.

Whatever differences of opinion existed in western Europe, Reagan was determined to press on with his assertive foreign policy. He was passionately anti-communist. Famously, in March 1983 he provocatively condemned the USSR as an 'evil empire' with ambitions to impose communism on the world and thus as a threat to world peace. He declared, however, 'Communism is another sad, bizarre chapter in human history whose last pages even now are being written.' He predicted that Marxism–Leninism would soon be left on 'the ash-heap of history'. Such rhetoric caused tremendous concern in Moscow. It was seen as indicating that Reagan intended to launch a nuclear war to turn the USSR into ashes.

As president from 1981, Reagan matched his fierce rhetoric with massive increases in US and NATO military spending — much of it on state-of-the-art weaponry that incorporated the latest computer technology. Most disturbingly from the Soviets' point of view was the launch of Reagan's futuristic **Strategic Defense Initiative** (SDI) of 1983, popularly known as 'Star Wars' after the series of movies of that name, which promised to neutralise the USSR's nuclear arsenal with a space-based anti-missiles system, thereby making the policy of Mutually Assured Destruction obsolete. In addition, the Reagan administration showed a new willingness to get directly involved in the struggle against communism in the developing world, for example in Grenada, Nicaragua and Africa, even when such actions were opposed by the United States Congress.

Reagan's fierce anti-Soviet rhetoric, his assertive foreign policy, and his administration's talk of the possibility of a 'limited' nuclear war, perhaps using neutron bombs, created panic in Moscow. It also caused widespread fears across Europe that Reagan was prepared to contemplate the possibility of war with the Soviet Union. The by then aged membership of the Politburo was extremely worried that Reagan was actually planning a nuclear war. The scale of the perceived threat to the survival of the Soviet Union was so great that it probably hastened the deaths of Brezhnev and his successors, Andropov and Chernenko, between 1982 and 1985. The NATO war game codenamed **Able Archer** in 1983 came very close to triggering a nuclear war when the Soviets' early-warning system mistakenly indicated that missiles had been launched from bases in the USA.

Knowledge check 40

Why were western European governments reluctant to voice their concerns in public about President Reagan's bellicose rhetoric and actions?

Strategic Defense Initiative A space-based anti-missiles platform that was promoted to the American public with state-of-the-art computer graphics.

Exam tip

President Reagan's foreign policy transformed relations between the Soviet Union and the western governments: be sure to give it due consideration in any essay on this unit.

Able Archer A NATO exercise designed to test its communications systems, which the Soviet leadership convinced themselves Reagan could use as a cover for a nuclear attack on the USSR.

The decline of the Soviet bloc, 1979–85

The threat posed by a resurgent USA under Ronald Reagan was compounded by economic decline across the Soviet bloc. The centrally controlled communist economies could not keep pace with the West. The Soviet system was being left behind by the 'Second Industrial Revolution', which was based on the rapid development of computer technology since the late 1970s. That weakness was massively compounded by the collapse in world oil prices in 1980, from $35 a barrel to less than $10. This had an enormous impact on the USSR because of its considerable dependence on oil revenues to finance federal government spending, 70 per cent of which comprised spending on the military.

The Soviets had also used oil to subsidise their satellite states, meaning those subsidies were now reduced across the Soviet bloc. Furthermore, foreign banks that had loaned money to eastern European governments, and thereby boosted economic activity across the region, now stopped providing loans because Soviet oil no longer provided sufficient collateral to guarantee them. In fact, foreign banks began to demand that existing loans be repaid. Poland alone owed $18 billion to western banks, and struggled to find the money to repay them.

Knowledge check 41
Why was the collapse in oil prices so catastrophic for the Soviet Union?

As a result of this, people's living standards, already very modest by western standards, fell sharply. The unrest this prompted, against the backdrop of decades of resentment of Soviet domination, was especially problematic in Poland, where the election of a Polish pope, John Paul II, gave the Poles the confidence to demand reforms. Large-scale strikes at the Lenin Shipyard in Gdansk in August and September 1980 escalated into a serious challenge to the communist system. The Polish government had no choice but to recognise the establishment of Solidarity, the first non-communist trade union in eastern Europe since the Second World War. Within a year Solidarity had 10 million members. Brezhnev reluctantly acquiesced to its existence for a time, because he was afraid that if the Red Army intervened in Poland, as it had done in Hungary in 1956 and Czechoslovakia in 1968, it might provoke the outbreak of a third world war given Reagan's fierce rhetoric. Nonetheless, in December 1981 Brezhnev forced the new Polish president, General Wojciech Jaruzelski, to ban the movement, or face the intervention of the Red Army.

The immediate crisis in Poland was defused, but the underlying economic problems across the Soviet bloc worsened steadily through the 1980s. In fact, Brezhnev and his immediate successors were entirely incapable of addressing the massive challenges facing the USSR in the 1980s from a combination of significant economic decline and grave insecurity.

The main events in Soviet foreign policy, 1985–91

Gorbachev

By 1985 even the Politburo recognised that the Soviet system needed systemic change, and it elected its youngest member, Mikhail Gorbachev, aged only 54, to reform Leninism inside the USSR. Gorbachev, however, had a 'vision but no strategy'.

He realised that major reforms were desirable and necessary, but did not engage in the systematic analysis and planning needed to achieve them.

The greatest challenge confronting the USSR when Gorbachev took power was economic: the fall in oil prices exposed its fundamental problems of low productivity and outdated technology. As living standards declined and the queues at shops for basic necessities grew, the credibility of communism was undermined. Gorbachev recognised the problem, in part from his trips overseas. He tried to revive the Soviet economy through an economic programme called *perestroika*, though it lacked precision or any kind of coherent practical strategy, unlike that the Chinese were adopting around the same time. He promoted greater openness or *glasnost*, which was partly intended to make the government, official institutions and services in the Soviet Union more accountable to public scrutiny. It was partly also because of a sincere belief that people ought to enjoy more freedom. Gorbachev hoped that this would improve standards.

Glasnost Greater openness, intended to release a greater sense of accountability in Soviet society and to spur productivity.

Andrei Grachev, one of Gorbachev's closest aides, explained that Gorbachev's foreign policy was motivated in part by economic considerations. He was driven by the desperate need to rescue the Soviet economy by cutting military spending and freeing up scarce resources that were needed for economic regeneration. Yet he was also motivated by a genuine commitment to peace and the belief that mankind had to find a way of living together peacefully because the alternative was unthinkable. Gorbachev believed in allowing people to enjoy greater democracy and responsibility for their own destinies. He nurtured a vision of a 'common European home', with relations between European states based on cooperation not coercion. At the same time, he remained a Leninist and was slow to see the implications for communism and the USSR of much that he did.

Soviet economic decline meant that the USSR simply could no longer afford to maintain its massive military spending — which accounted for 70 per cent of the state budget — or to keep subsidising its many poor or impoverished client satellites around the world. There was a growing feeling in Moscow that the Soviet Union had over-reached itself in the Brezhnev era in terms of its ideological commitments, and that it needed to retrench and focus on its own survival. Also, it could not support the astronomical costs of a new arms race, and its technology was very outdated in any case. For the sake of its own self-preservation Gorbachev realised that he had to get the Soviet Union out of the Cold War.

Thawing of tensions

Gorbachev found that Reagan was anxious for nuclear disarmament, even if he had no clear ideas how to achieve it. The two leaders met at Geneva in November 1985 and talked vaguely about it. Despite the lack of solid progress, there was a palpable thawing of tensions between the two superpowers. Oil prices fell by two-thirds in 1985–86, putting additional huge pressure on Gorbachev to extricate the Soviet Union from the Cold War. In October 1986, at a conference at Reykjavik, Gorbachev proposed the 'zero option' — no superpower nuclear weapons in Europe, if Reagan would agree to abandon his 'Star Wars' project. The US president was too wedded to his idea to agree, but he recognised the opportunity to make real progress in limiting the threat from nuclear weapons. One year later, at Washington, the two sides agreed to remove all

Knowledge check 42

What motivated Gorbachev to massively reduce the Soviet Union's nuclear and conventional military forces?

intermediate-range missiles from Europe, including the SS20 and Pershing missiles. In a unilateral move Gorbachev cut the size of the Red Army massively, reducing it by 500,000 soldiers in 1987 alone, and withdrew it from Afghanistan in 1988.

End of the Cold War

In his book *Perestroika* (1987), Gorbachev presented his vision of a better world in keeping with his belief in freedom. The logic of his words was the abandonment of the use of coercion to maintain the Soviet empire. In 1989 his Foreign Minister, Eduard Shevardnadze, declared that the Soviet Union had abandoned the Brezhnev Doctrine for the '**Sinatra doctrine**', named after the extremely popular American singer Frank Sinatra. Hesitantly at first, the peoples of eastern Europe tested his sincerity. Starting in Poland and Hungary, communist control all over the region crumbled without a guarantee of Red Army support. Gorbachev announced that the peoples of eastern Europe were free to 'seek their own destinies', and by Christmas 1989 all of the communist regimes in eastern Europe were gone. President Gorbachev and President George H.W. Bush met at Malta in December 1989 and announced that the Cold War was over.

End of the USSR

Despite the end of communism in eastern Europe, Gorbachev still hoped to secure the future of the USSR without resorting to violence or the threat of violence. He was genuinely convinced that it was in the best interests of the peoples of the Soviet Union to stay together. The transition from communist state-controlled economics towards market forces proved disastrous, however. After registering a miserly 1.5 per cent growth in GNP in 1989, the USSR's GNP declined by a catastrophic 12 per cent in 1990 and by another 13 per cent in 1991. The peoples of the USSR found themselves free-falling into dire straits. **Life expectancy** fell for the first time in decades: for men from 65 years in 1987 to 57 years in 1994, for women from 74.3 to 72.

Consequently, while Gorbachev was widely praised in the West for his heroic efforts to reform the Soviet Union, at home he was generally hated. The absolute failure of his economic reforms, combined with the revelations about the Stalinist past and the freedoms Gorbachev gave the people to voice their dissatisfaction, undermined the Communist Party of the Soviet Union. Nationalism made itself heard again, especially in the Baltic states but not just there. Early in 1991 Lithuania declared its independence, followed by its neighbours.

Nonetheless, the greatest challenge to the unity of the Soviet Union came from its centre. As part of his campaign for greater democracy and accountability, Gorbachev established a Russian government that was responsible to a democratically elected Russian parliament or duma. That had the result that by July 1991 there was a Russian president, Boris Yeltsin, who had a popular mandate — whereas Gorbachev, the Soviet president, had none. In August 1991 some senior communist hardliners staged a coup, convinced that Gorbachev was destroying the Soviet Union. Gorbachev was put under house arrest. President Yeltsin, however, saved the day. He took charge in Moscow to popular acclaim, and the coup disintegrated. Yeltsin consolidated his victory by banning the Communist Party of the Soviet Union (CPSU), Gorbachev's powerbase.

Exam tip

You must acknowledge the contribution of both Gorbachev and Reagan to the thawing of tensions.

'Sinatra doctrine' One of the most popular songs in the repertoire of Frank Sinatra was 'My way'. The 'Sinatra doctrine' made it clear that the states of eastern Europe were free to go their own ways.

Life expectancy A statistical measure of how long an average person can expect to live. It is a crude measure of the quality of life in an area.

Knowledge check 43

What made President Yeltsin such a formidable rival to President Gorbachev?

Over the final months of 1991 Gorbachev tried desperately to devise a formula to hold the 15 republics of the USSR together in some kind of federal arrangement. A referendum in October 1991 showed that most citizens in Russia, and in several of the other Soviet republics, wanted the Soviet Union to survive in some form. Yeltsin, however, had a vision of a democratic and capitalist Russia with no place for Gorbachev. In early December 1991 Yeltsin and the presidents of Ukraine and Belarus formed the Commonwealth of Independent States, and then announced to President Bush that the Soviet Union was no more. Gorbachev was shocked at their treachery, but on Christmas Day 1991 he accepted the new reality and formally dissolved the USSR. Boris Yeltsin took charge in the Kremlin as the president of an independent Russia.

Western governments, 1979–91

Ronald Reagan was elected to be the USA's president in 1980 (taking office in 1981) with a mission to end the Cold War through an outright victory by the USA over the USSR. By 1989, just one year after the end of his presidency, Reagan's aim was achieved. Reagan was motivated by a fierce hostility to communism. That can be traced back to the late 1940s when he denounced several of his fellow actors to the FBI as 'communist sympathisers'. In his election campaign in 1980 he castigated President Jimmy Carter as weak and as having allowed the Soviets to take advantage of Détente to strengthen Soviet power and communist ideology around the globe. Reagan set out to reverse the Soviet gains.

Reagan aimed to build up the USA's military power to enhance its security, and to curtail any further ambitions of the Soviet Union. In his first year as president US military spending was increased by a massive 13 per cent, and by 10 per cent per annum thereafter. Much of the money was invested in state-of-the-art weapons that used the latest computer technology being developed in the USA, most notably cruise and Pershing missiles, and the incredibly expensive Stealth Bomber planes (each of which cost $737 million in 1997). Reagan pushed military technology to its very limits, and beyond, in his Strategic Defense Initiative (SDI), which promised to neutralise the Soviet Union's nuclear arsenal before it could harm the USA. At the same time, the Reagan administration asserted American power more aggressively against Soviet client states in the Third World, most notably against Grenada and Nicaragua and in southern Africa.

This huge investment in the American military coincided with rapid economic growth in the USA, based partly on massive federal state borrowing but also on American manufacturers having become more competitive through the development of new technologies, and through the exploitation of new sources of oil in the USA itself. By 1983 Reagan felt that he had achieved most of what he set out to do: to make the USA great again, to rebuild its military and to reverse the threat from the USSR/communism.

After learning how close the world came to a nuclear war during the NATO exercise Able Archer (see page 53) and having watched *The Day After*, a movie about the aftermath of a nuclear war, Reagan decided that it was time to de-escalate the Cold War. He wrote in his diary, 'I feel that the Soviets are so defense-minded, so paranoid about being attacked that without in any way being soft on them we ought to tell them that no one here has any intention of doing anything like that. What the hell have they

Knowledge check 44

Why could the USSR not compete with the USA in the arms race initiated by President Reagan?

got that anyone would want?' In addition, Reagan was coming under pressure from anti-war movements across western Europe in the early to mid-1980s to stop pursuing a nuclear arms race that was persuading most Europeans that a nuclear war was being made inevitable. Hence, when he met Gorbachev at Geneva in October 1985 he let the Soviet leader know that he was keen to prevent the outbreak of a nuclear war.

While western European governments were very enthusiastic from the start about Gorbachev's reformist agenda, and ordinary people were very enthusiastic about his calls to end the Cold War, Reagan was cautious while he waited to see substantial changes being made by the Soviet leader. Gorbachev's offer of the 'zero option' at Reykjavik in October 1986 turned out to be a breakthrough moment. Momentum was generated, which led to agreement a year later on the elimination of intermediate-range nuclear missiles from Europe.

However, even though Gorbachev explained to President Reagan that his reforms inside the USSR needed external support in order to succeed, the Americans were reluctant to help the USSR. They continued to provide weapons to the Mujahideen, the Islamic fundamentalists who fought the Red Army in Afghanistan. Reagan's successor as president, George H. W. Bush, was even more reluctant to help Gorbachev, because he still saw the Soviet Union as the USA's main rival in the world. Hence, the Americans stood by passively as the Soviet economy spiralled towards collapse.

The collapse of the Soviet bloc across eastern Europe forced Bush to meet with Gorbachev in December 1989, to bring stability to a situation that was fraught with uncertainty. The two leaders publicly announced that the Cold War was over, but Gorbachev was disappointed to discover that Bush still wanted to pursue the USA's ideological enemies in Cuba and Nicaragua. Bush offered some vague promises of help to boost trade to aid the Soviet economy, but offered nothing concrete. Yet President Bush disagreed with some of his own advisers, who wanted to see the break-up of the Soviet Union to guarantee the USA's predominance in the world forever. The president was anxious lest the break-up of the USSR generate instability, especially around the mainly Muslim republics in Asia. In 1990 Bush publicly declared that Washington did not want to see the disintegration of the USSR, a message he reiterated in Ukraine in 1991.

German reunification

The main concern of the western governments in the immediate aftermath of the fall of communism in eastern Europe was the future of Germany. West German Chancellor Helmut Kohl recognised the fall of the Berlin Wall as a once-in-a-lifetime opportunity to reunite the two Germanies. Britain's Mrs Thatcher, however, did not want to see Germany enlarged and dominant in the middle of Europe. She stoked French and Soviet anxieties to try to block **German reunification**. Nonetheless, reunification became inevitable after more than 40 per cent of East Germans voted for Kohl's Christian Democrat Party in the country's first democratic election, and East Germany's economy started to collapse as its own citizens stopped buying its products once they could buy freely from the West. Gorbachev bowed to the inevitable and worked with Bush and Kohl, along with a petulant Thatcher and a less-than-enthusiastic French President Mitterrand, to see Germany united by October 1990.

German reunification Achieved after the first democratic election was held in East Germany in March 1990. The former East German Communist Party secured only 16.4% of the vote, and there was an overwhelming majority in favour of reunification.

The French and Germans worked together to integrate the new Germany more fully into a wider European Community, while all of Germany became part of the American-led NATO. The German Question was finally resolved. The other great problem of post-Cold War Europe, the break-up of **Yugoslavia**, however, was not resolved successfully. Instead there was a series of mini-wars and a great deal of ethnic cleansing as the nationalities of the former Serb-dominated state wrenched themselves apart over a decade from 1990.

After the USSR

As the Soviet Union itself disintegrated in the second half of 1991 western governments were all verbally supportive of Gorbachev's efforts at reform, but none could save either the Soviet economy or the Soviet Union. The dissolution of the USSR in December 1991 was accepted as a fait accompli. The European Union became ever more integrated, and it expanded eastwards to incorporate the eastern European states that had been subject to Soviet domination after the Second World War, in order to foster political stability, civil liberty and economic prosperity across the continent. NATO too was expanded to incorporate the eastern European states and the Baltic states, which were fearful of Russian revenge at any point in the future.

The clash of ideologies in Europe was over. Communism disappeared all across Europe, having been completely discredited. The USSR was gone, and its nuclear arsenal and conventional forces were cut massively. In fact, Russia's economy remained in crisis until Vladimir Putin resuscitated it in the early twenty-first century. The USA was the clear winner of the Cold War.

The successes and failures of Soviet foreign policy, 1917–91

If one looks at Soviet foreign policy across the course of the history of the USSR it seems obvious that its failures were far greater than its successes. Its ideological ambition to spread communism beyond its borders was seen as a threat by all of the more advanced countries in the world, and as such made enemies of them. Hence, for much of its existence the Soviet Union was isolated in international relations and vulnerable to the possibility of attack. Its foreign policy was focused mainly on the aim of protecting the USSR and keeping it out of war with powerful ideological foes, until the 'World Revolution' predicted by Karl Marx materialised. Its efforts to achieve security were undermined, however, by its continuing, underlying ambition to spread communism. Those unresolved tensions in Soviet foreign policy led to its failure, at least until Gorbachev, the last Soviet leader, abandoned any ambition to impose communist ideology outside its borders.

Lenin's foreign policy shifted dramatically during his time as Russia's leader, reflecting the fact that it failed repeatedly. His initial expectations of a spontaneous 'World Revolution' were soon disappointed, and his efforts to support revolutionary movements outside of Russia — in Finland, the Baltic states and Germany — all ended in failure. His attempt to promote revolutions through Comintern failed. His efforts to use the Red Army to make Poland a 'red bridge' to the rest of Europe failed. Lenin enjoyed a little success when he changed his foreign policy in 1921 in order to develop trade to boost the NEP, but apart from the Treaty of Rapello it was a very insubstantial success.

Yugoslavia A country formed by the extension of Serbian control over a large part of the territories of the former Austro-Hungarian empire in the Balkans in 1918. It became a non-aligned communist state under Josip Tito in 1946, but after Tito's death in 1980 and the collapse of communism elsewhere in Europe, the country started to disintegrate, with each of its different nationalities forming their own separate states.

Stalin was probably the first foreign leader to realise the nature of the threat posed by Hitler. Despite his earnest efforts, however, his foreign policy failed to achieve the 'collective security' that Stalin sought. His 'Terror' inside the USSR, and his ideological ambitions, made him seem more threatening than Hitler. The Nazi–Soviet Pact of August 1939 reflects the failure of his foreign policy. The pact itself was disastrous. It allowed Hitler to conquer western Europe with impunity in 1940, before concentrating almost all of Germany's forces against the Soviet Union in June of the following year. Operation Barbarossa very nearly succeeded because the Soviets were left to fight the Germans virtually alone.

One could argue that Stalin's foreign policy was more successful after the war. He was able to impose Soviet power on eastern Europe, and maintained it in the face of American opposition. His efforts to promote Soviet influence and communism beyond the Iron Curtain failed in the face of a determined American policy of containment, however. Though Stalin was astute enough not to force the Berlin Blockade to the point of war, Cold War tensions were ratcheted up to a dangerous level before he died. The collective leadership that succeeded Stalin recognised his foreign policy was counterproductive in the sense that by projecting Soviet strength he caused an American reaction and thus aggravated the Cold War.

Khrushchev's foreign policy of 'peaceful coexistence' was well conceived, and succeeded in creating a 'thaw' in the Cold War. It brought stability to East–West relations in Europe, but no resolution to the Cold War. In fact, the crushing of the Hungarian Uprising in 1956 was a major setback for Khrushchev's foreign policy. It undid much of the progress he had made in improving relations with the USA and western Europe. More importantly, it reflected the failure of his foreign policy aspiration to base Soviet influence in eastern Europe on anything other than the threat of military intervention. That grave weakness in Soviet foreign policy was exposed again under Brezhnev during the 'Prague Spring'.

The Brezhnev era seemed to be characterised mostly by foreign policy successes for the USSR, but in fact much of this success was the result of temporary American weakness. Brezhnev's expansion of Soviet power and communist ideology in the Third World proved extremely costly for the USSR, both politically and economically. On the one hand, it helped Ronald Reagan become elected as the US president in 1980 on a fiercely anti-Soviet platform, and allowed him to get the approval of Congress for massively increased funding for the 'Second Cold War'. On the other hand, the Soviet Union became dangerously over-extended in terms of the costs of maintaining its enlarged empire and its many dependent client states. The Soviet system proved incapable of coping with the challenges posed by President Reagan's bellicose threats and his massive military build-up, coinciding as it did with a growing economic crisis in the USSR that was exacerbated by the Soviet Union's inability to gain access to the new technologies being developed in the West, and the drain of all the demands involved in maintaining its 'red empire'.

Gorbachev succeeded through his foreign policy in ending the Cold War, and ending with it the threat of the nuclear holocaust that was widely feared in the 1980s. He failed, however, to win the economic support he desperately needed from the West to transform the Soviet Union, or even to hold it together. In December 1991 the USSR simply fell apart.

All in all, Soviet foreign policy must be judged to have been characterised more by failure than success, despite its apparent successes after the Second World War.

Exam tip

The fact that CCEA includes a section on 'successes and failures' in the specification for this unit shows that it considers it important. Be well prepared by planning for and practising writing an essay on that subject.

Summary

- After the strong American reaction to the Red Army's intervention in Afghanistan, the Soviet Politburo found itself unexpectedly in a 'Second Cold War'.
- The Soviet Union could not match the massive arms build-up initiated by President Ronald Reagan in the USA and the USA's allies in NATO, and the Politburo was panicked by Reagan's fierce anti-Soviet rhetoric.
- By 1985 the Politburo recognised that the economic crisis within the USSR, and the threat posed to its security by Reagan's America, necessitated radical changes in the Soviet system.
- Mikhail Gorbachev recognised the need for reform, but he had no clear or effective programme to revive the Soviet economy.
- Gorbachev was extremely popular in the West for his efforts to end the Cold War and promote greater freedom in the Soviet bloc, but as the Soviet economy lurched deeper into crisis he was increasingly reviled at home.
- The end of Soviet control over eastern Europe was permitted in order to end the Cold War and to divert desperately needed resources to prop up the ailing Soviet economy, but also because Gorbachev sincerely believed that people were entitled to the freedom to choose their own destinies.
- The failure of Gorbachev's economic policies, together with the greater openness and democracy he allowed within the USSR, led to the collapse of the USSR itself by December 1991.

Questions & Answers

How to use this section

This section includes a guide to the structure of the examination for CCEA's A2 Paper 1 History, Option 5: Clash of ideologies in Europe 1900–2000, including an explanation of the assessment objective examined by the paper. It is important that you familiarise yourself with both the exam structure and the nature of the assessment objective.

There follows a specimen exam paper with sample answers. The questions are neither past examination questions nor future examination questions, but they are similar to the kind of questions you will face.

The best way to use this section of the guide is to look at each question and make notes on how you would go about answering it, including the key facts and knowledge you would use, any arguments you would deploy and the conclusions you would reach. You should also make a plan of how you would answer the whole question, taking account of any tips (indicated by the icon ⓔ) immediately below the question.

For each specimen question given, there is an exemplar answer. The strengths of each specimen answer are explained in the commentary (indicated by the icon ⓔ). Compare these specimen answers with your own notes. Amend your notes to bring them to the standard of the specimen. Having done all this, you can now attempt a full answer to the question, including the strengths that have been indicated in the specimen answer.

Of course, the guidance offered is merely a recommendation. You must take responsibility for your own work. Use the guidance to help you learn and practise *how* to answer questions 'actively' — that is, by writing your own answers and using the questions and specimen answers as guides. In this way you will be able to effectively tackle *any* questions that may come your way in the examination. Simply 'learning' specimen answers will not be sufficient to do well in A-level History — no one but the examiner knows what precise questions you will have to tackle in your actual examination!

The structure of the examination

A2 History Paper 1

This unit is examined in a one-hour examination. You must answer a synoptic essay question, covering a period of approximately 100 years and worth 40 marks. You must answer **one** question from a choice of two. You will have **one hour** to write your answer.

The synoptic essay on Clash of ideologies in Europe 1900–2000 tests your ability to assess change and/or development in the foreign policies of the USSR and those of western governments in the twentieth century, to demonstrate your understanding of the process of historical change.

AO1

The synoptic essay question assesses Assessment Object 1 (AO1). For AO1, you are expected to demonstrate, organise and communicate knowledge and understanding, in order to analyse and evaluate the key features related to the foreign policies of the USSR and the important western governments as outlined in CCEA's specification, making substantiated judgements and exploring, as relevant, concepts of cause, consequence, change, continuity, similarity, difference and significance.

Advice

The synoptic essay poses a number of challenges, not least the real difficulty of discussing a subject as complex as the often adversarial foreign policy relationships of the USSR and the western governments — and to do so in an essay for which you have one hour only. The examiners are looking for comprehensive coverage of the period in question, with detailed analysis and substantiated conclusions. Success will depend on you having deep knowledge of the subject, and also the ability to address a range of questions about the foreign policies of the countries on either side of the ideological divide in Europe. You have to be sensitive to the changes in foreign policy, whether prompted by changing circumstances or by the choices made by political leaders.

The most important advice anyone can offer is to **make sure that you answer the precise question asked**. It is stating the obvious, but it is all too often forgotten under examination conditions. Because the volume of material to be mastered is so great, and the time allocated for the examination is so short, there is a temptation simply to present a summary of the main events without analysis or explanation. In fact, the worst mistake a student can possibly make is to answer an examination question by regurgitating a memorised generic essay. The synoptic paper is designed to test your knowledge and understanding of specific topics; it is not a memory test. Bear in mind that this paper is worth 40 per cent of your A2 History grade — it has to be earned.

It is obviously very important that you complete your answer to your choice of question posed in this examination. A strong essay will never lack a conclusion. For this particular unit, with such a great volume of content to consider in such a limited timeframe, it will be no small challenge to get your timing right. Nevertheless, before you start writing your answer, take time to read the questions carefully and ensure that you understand clearly what each is asking. Think about your answer, what you will argue, the knowledge relevant to your answer, and the structure you will use to present your answer to best effect.

Practise addressing essay questions on this unit within a one-hour timeframe. Note how much time it takes you to reach specific key points in the course of the twentieth century, for example how long it takes you to begin your discussion of foreign policies in Europe from the time of Hitler's accession to power, from the end of the Second World War, from the Soviet intervention in Afghanistan or from Gorbachev becoming the leader of the USSR. Keep a close eye on your timing throughout the exam to ensure that you write the best answer you are capable of presenting.

■ Sample paper

You have to answer either Question 1 or Question 2.

Question 1

1 **How far was the conflict in Europe between the Soviet Union and the western governments between 1917 and 1991 due to their opposing political ideologies?**　　　　　　　　　　　　　　　　　　**(40 marks)**

ⓔ The key to success with this unit is to answer the precise question asked, and not present the answer to a similar question. The worst mistake a student can make is to answer a question from a past paper instead of addressing the question posed on the examination paper in front of you. Any hint that you are regurgitating a pre-prepared answer will be heavily penalised. Take particular care not to repeat key words or phrases from past paper questions: focus on the precise wording of the question you are answering.

ⓔ Examiners expect every student to know more than enough facts to address any question about the 'Clash of Ideologies'. They are not looking for a simple summary of the main events. What they look for, especially from students hoping to achieve top grades, is a clear, well-substantiated argument, where information is used to support and illustrate the point being made. It is important that you think about different possible interpretations of the evidence while studying this unit. The examiners are particularly generous towards students who show some degree of originality and flair in their essays. The best way to develop such flair is by reading around the subject and making up your own mind.

Student answer

I believe that the conflict between the Soviet Union and the western governments was primarily due to their opposing ideologies, though not exclusively so. The Soviet leadership saw themselves as the vanguard in a Marxist-inspired 'World Revolution' that would overthrow the capitalist governments in the West. Western governments, in turn, were opposed to Marxist ideology and were anxious to neutralise threats posed by the Soviet Red Army and from Soviet-backed communist insurgents outside the USSR. It was not so much the opposing ideologies that caused most of the tensions in Europe in this period, however, as the perceived level of threat posed by one side or the other, so there were long periods of relatively peaceful coexistence as well as periods of conflict.

ⓔ When choosing which question to answer, consider not only what you know about the subject but, no less importantly, how well you can present a substantiated argument about it. Where possible, choose the question for which it is easiest for you to debate different possible answers. In this case, the argument is that the occasions of greatest conflict were caused not simply by the existence of ideological differences, but also by the attempts by one side or the other to challenge its ideological rival(s).

The Bolsheviks' commitment to 'World Revolution' was the major source of conflict with the West. At first the Bolsheviks expected revolutions to occur spontaneously. The Decree on Peace (Oct. 1917) and the Treaty of Brest-Litovsk (March 1918) were pragmatic choices to secure the Bolshevik regime until revolutions erupted elsewhere. When revolutions did not occur, Lenin supported communist insurgents in Finland, the Baltic states, Germany, Hungary and Italy. In March 1919 the Bolsheviks established Comintern to promote 'World Revolution'. In August 1920 Lenin went one step further and used the Red Army to try to make Poland a 'red bridge' into Europe.

Western governments, in turn, felt threatened by the Bolsheviks' active support for 'World Revolution'. That was of greater concern than their anger about the Bolsheviks taking Russia out of the First World War against Germany, and confiscating the assets of western capitalists. Many western governments intervened in the Russian Civil War against the Reds, but they did not fight directly. Churchill later regretted that the West failed to 'strangle Bolshevism at birth'.

e The role of opposing political ideologies in causing conflict is made clear from the start.

By 1921 western fears of the USSR subsided as communists failed to seize power outside of Russia, and the Red Army was routed by the Poles near Warsaw. Ideological tensions persisted, as shown by the exclusion of the Soviet Union from the Paris peace settlements and from membership of the League of Nations, but both sides were careful not to allow those tensions to escalate into armed conflict. In fact, when Lenin sought improved relations with the West to improve the USSR's security and bolster his NEP from 1921, several western governments agreed to make trade deals with the Soviets. Germany, Europe's other pariah state, responded very positively with the Treaty of Rapello in 1922. The response to Lenin's appeal for a rapprochement with the West shows that it was not simply the existence of opposing ideologies that generated conflict, but the level of threat posed by the USSR. Yet, despite an improvement in East–West relations, ideological tensions persisted beneath the surface.

e The argument is made that ideological differences alone did not cause the greatest conflict, but rather the attempt of one side or the other to impose its ideology on its rivals.

Soviet–western relations were characterised by continuity throughout the 1920s, reflected in Chicherin remaining as the Soviet Commissar for Foreign Affairs after Lenin's death. Stalin's 'Socialism in one country' emphasised domestic priorities rather than ideological ambitions. The Soviets' passivity in foreign affairs encouraged western governments in turn to ignore the USSR. They were more concerned with the rehabilitation of Germany and the economic challenges of the inter-war years than with ideological conflicts.

Stalin, however, was convinced that military conflict with the capitalist West was inevitable, because of their opposing ideologies. The Five Year Plans of his

'Second Revolution', ostensibly launched to create a socialist society, were, in fact, focused on the 'sinews of war'. Stalin commented in 1931 that the Soviet economy was a hundred years behind the West — they had to catch up in ten 'or go under'.

Hitler coming to power in Germany in 1933 greatly intensified the ideological contest in Europe. Hitler's *Mein Kampf* showed that he had a pathological hatred of 'Judeo-Bolshevism', but it also showed that his ambitions were not just anti-communist — he wanted to conquer *Lebensraum* in the East for his 'master race'. The coming conflict in Europe was not simply about a clash of ideologies. Stalin responded by intensifying the FYPs and the build-up of the Red Army, and by seeking 'collective security'. The USSR joined the League of Nations (1934), and formed alliances with France (1935) and Czechoslovakia (1935). Soviet efforts to form a 'Popular Front' against the Fascists failed, however, because so many democrats regarded communist ideology as more threatening than Fascism to the existing order. When the USSR intervened in the Spanish Civil War against the Fascist-backed Nationalists in 1936–39, Britain and France remained neutral. They were more worried about communists taking power in Spain than Franco.

e The intensification of ideological rivalry between the communists and their enemies is highlighted, but also the complication of a three-fold ideological division across Europe in the 1930s.

Stalin recognised that the ideological divisions in Europe — between the democracies, the Fascists and the Soviets — facilitated German ambitions. The Anti-Comintern Pact (1936) worsened that threat. Hence Stalin disengaged from Spain in the hope that a Fascist victory there might encourage Britain and France to ally with the USSR. The exclusion of the USSR from the Munich Conference (Sept. 1938), however, suggested to Stalin that Britain's and France's foreign policies were encouraging Hitler eastwards to save their own skins. Therefore, when his efforts to form an anti-German pact failed in the summer of 1939, Stalin agreed to a Nazi–Soviet Pact (August 1939) in what seemed like a pragmatic move to keep the USSR out of a general European war while it was vulnerable. That shows that even the most fiercely opposing political ideologies did not necessarily cause conflict when governments had other priorities.

e The Nazi–Soviet Pact is the best demonstration that the existence of opposing political ideologies by themselves did not make conflict inevitable.

Stalin's ideological ambitions were exposed when he expanded Soviet power into eastern Poland, the Baltic states, Finland and Bessarabia in 1939/40. He hoped that war between the western governments would lead to communist revolutions. After Hitler's stunning victories in the West, however, the Germans invaded the USSR in Operation Barbarossa (June 1941). The result over the following four years was the most savage war in history. Yet although it was certainly a war of opposing ideologies, much of the savagery arose from Hitler's concept of a 'war of annihilation' to free up *Lebensraum* for his supposed 'master race', and the non-communist Poles were as much victims of Hitler's racism as the citizens of the Soviet Union.

e Again, the argument is made that opposing political ideologies do not fully explain the greatest conflict in Europe in the twentieth century.

After Hitler declared war on the USA in December 1941 the USSR, USA and UK formed a Grand Alliance against Nazi Germany. That again demonstrates that opposing ideologies did not necessarily make conflict inevitable. Nonetheless, though their ideological differences were set to one side during the war on Nazi Germany, relations between the Allies were often strained. Stalin was convinced that the Americans and British were happy for the USSR to bear the brunt of the war for the selfish reason of minimising their own casualties. To his mind, the long-delayed 'second front' only materialised on D-Day 1944 because the USA and UK did not want the Soviets to extend communism over all of Europe. Hence, though the Allies hoped that the Grand Alliance could maintain the postwar settlement, there was a high probability that their opposing ideologies would generate conflict in Europe once their common aim of destroying Nazism was achieved.

e The setting aside of ideological differences by the members of the Grand Alliance reinforces the argument that those differences by themselves did not necessarily cause conflict, though they certainly complicated an already strained relationship between the 'Big Three'.

The direct involvement of the USA in European affairs was a major development in postwar foreign policy. American policy was profoundly shaped by hostility to communist ideology. It was also designed to serve other American interests, however, by maintaining stability in the postwar world, its new status as the world's greatest power, and its economic interests. It was not motivated solely by ideology. Nonetheless, President Truman's thinking was shaped by George Kennan's 'Long Telegram', which warned that the USSR was inherently expansionist both for ideological reasons and to enhance Russia's security. The Soviets had already established a 'buffer zone' in eastern Europe, and expected Germany to become communist 'at any second'. Communist insurgents were fighting in Greece, and the Soviets were putting pressure on Turkey. The Truman Doctrine of March 1947 was a public declaration of the US commitment to containing what was seen as a direct threat to the West from the USSR and from the communist insurgents it sponsored.

e Emphasis is placed on the USA's range of motives, but especially on the perceived threat posed by Stalin's USSR.

Stalin's postwar policy was shaped by his view that the existence of opposing political ideologies made conflict inevitable, as he stated in February 1946. Soviet foreign policy was more concerned about security than about spreading communism, however. That was understandable after the 27 million deaths and incredible economic losses it suffered in the war. As Truman engaged in 'atomic diplomacy' and withheld financial aid because of Stalin's non-fulfilment of the Declaration on Liberated Europe, relations between Moscow and the West deteriorated.

The Truman Doctrine of March 1947 heightened the ideological tensions between East and West by making them explicit. Marshall Aid was seen by the Soviets as the Americans using their economic muscle to increase their control over western Europe, so they responded by tightening their grip over eastern Europe through Cominform. The West's rebuilding of the German economy caused alarm in the USSR, but Stalin's response, the Berlin Blockade (1948/9), brought the ideological contest between East and West very close to actual warfare. It was probably the USA's monopoly of the atomic bomb that ensured that there was no World War III. Nonetheless, in a sign that he was prepared to compromise his ideological principles for the sake of Soviet security, the 'Stalin Note' offered to give up communist East Germany if a reunited Germany was kept disarmed and neutral forever. This is more evidence that opposing ideologies did not have to lead to conflict.

e The immediate postwar period was very eventful, and ideological tensions were high. Yet the 'Stalin Note' is cited as evidence that conflict could be avoided despite the existence of opposing ideologies.

Stalin's death led to a 'thaw' in the Cold War. Without him the Politburo hoped to de-escalate the Cold War, believing that opposing political ideologies need not lead to conflict. They offered the 'Stalin Note' again to solve the German Question and in 1955 they withdrew the Red Army from Austria to prove their lack of expansionist ambitions. At Geneva the new Soviet leader, Khrushchev, announced his desire for 'peaceful coexistence', meaning that the two opposing ideological systems could coexist in peaceful competition.

e Again, the point is emphasised that conflict was not inevitable despite the existence of opposing political ideologies.

Nonetheless, tensions between East and West persisted because the new American president, Ike Eisenhower, was fiercely hostile to communist ideology. It was the era of 'McCarthyism' in the USA. Arguably, an opportunity to end the Cold War was lost. Khrushchev was keen to divert spending away from the military and into the economy and improved living standards. Instead, both sides engaged in an arms race and the Space Race, which kept the conflict alive.

Khrushchev was forced to react to developments that threatened the Soviet 'empire' and communist ideology: West Germany's integration into NATO in 1955; Imre Nagy's announcement that Hungary would hold free elections and leave the Warsaw Pact in November 1956; the dispute about West Berlin in 1958–61. Nonetheless, none of these challenges led to open conflict with the West because, despite Eisenhower's rhetoric about 'roll-back', neither the western governments nor the Politburo wanted to risk a nuclear war. Both sides accepted that they would have to coexist despite their opposing ideologies, because the alternative was MAD!

e Given the constraints of time it is necessary to make just cursory references to some of the events of the period covered in this unit.

Brezhnev took power in 1964. His priority was to avoid direct conflict with the West while the Soviet Union invested in achieving nuclear parity with the USA in order to ensure its security. Despite the embarrassment of having to deploy Warsaw Pact forces to crush the 'Prague Spring' in 1968, Brezhnev's foreign policy was characterised by Détente, the reduction of tensions between East and West. It was a policy that was embraced by both sides of the ideological divide. Both superpowers, and their satellites in Europe, agreed that opposing political ideologies need not cause conflict. West Germany's Chancellor, Willy Brandt, was especially keen with his *Ostpolitik*. The German Question seemed to be resolved by the Quadripartite Protocol on Germany (1971). The Helsinki Accords (1975) promised political stability across Europe, and greater freedom and more rights behind the Iron Curtain. SALT 1 (1972) marked progress in reducing the threat of nuclear war. Until the Soviet intervention in Afghanistan in 1979 it seemed that the supporters of the opposing political ideologies in Europe had found a modus vivendi.

e The Brezhnev era up to 1979 tallies best with the argument being presented in this essay.

During Détente Brezhnev took advantage of US weakness — caused by a combination of failing confidence due to the Vietnam War and repeated oil crises and recession — to expand Soviet influence in the Third World. That was partly a matter of prestige and partly a response to Chinese competition for leadership of the communist world, and not simply ideological ambition. The Soviet intervention in Afghanistan was seen as a step too far by the Americans, however. Starting with President Carter, but more fiercely under President Reagan, it sparked off a 'Second Cold War'. Reagan used extraordinarily violent rhetoric against the 'evil empire' and prompted massive increases in American and NATO military spending, much of it on state-of-the-art cruise and Pershing missiles. Reagan's SDI ('Star Wars') threatened to neutralise the Soviet nuclear arsenal and the policy of MAD. The Soviet Politburo was convinced that Reagan intended to plunge the world into a nuclear war because of their opposing ideologies. Their anxiety contributed to the deaths of Brezhnev, Andropov and Chernenko in quick succession in 1982–85.

On becoming the Soviet leader in 1985 Mikhail Gorbachev recognised that the 'Second Cold War' was disastrous for the Soviet Union, economically and in terms of its security. He adopted a new foreign policy to extricate the USSR from the Cold War. He believed that there was no reason why opposing political ideologies should lead to conflict with the West. He abandoned the USSR's commitment to supporting communist ideology beyond its frontiers, because the political and economic costs were prohibitive. He called for nuclear disarmament at Geneva (Nov. 1985) and at Reykjavik (Oct. 1986), and finally achieved it at Malta in December 1989. He withdrew the Red Army from Afghanistan late in 1988, and cut the army greatly in size. He abandoned the Brezhnev Doctrine for the 'Sinatra doctrine', and allowed the peoples of eastern Europe to 'seek their own destinies'. By the end of 1989 all of the communist regimes in eastern Europe had been ousted. In all of these actions Gorbachev was true to his belief that opposing ideologies could coexist peacefully in Europe.

e Make sure that you leave sufficient time to discuss the significance of Gorbachev's term of office for the question you are answering. Avoid the temptation simply to bullet-point the main events. In this case, what do they tell us about opposing political ideologies and conflict?

The failings of *perestroika* and the revelations about the Stalinist 'Terror' under *glasnost* undermined the authority of the CPSU, however. Nationalism made itself heard again in the republics of the USSR. Despite Gorbachev's efforts to promote a mixed economy and greater democracy — through the Soviet Congress of Peoples' Deputies (1989) and the Russian duma (1990) — the USSR collapsed on Christmas Day 1991.

e Make sure you write a conclusion that encapsulates your argument in a nutshell.

It can be seen that the opposing ideologies of the Soviet Union and the western governments generated considerable tensions in Europe from 1917 to 1991. Nonetheless, those ideological differences did not by themselves lead to open conflicts. Conflicts arose when one side or the other threatened the security of its ideological rivals. For most of the twentieth century the two ideological camps were able to coexist in a strained, yet stable, peace.

e This sample essay ought to achieve a top grade since it addresses the question directly, deploys relevant and precise historical knowledge, shows deep understanding of the subject, and offers a well-substantiated judgement in the conclusion.

Question 2

2 'The death of Stalin in 1953 marked the most important turning point in relations between the Soviet Union and western governments in Europe in the period 1917–91.' To what extent would you accept this verdict? **(40 marks)**

ⓔ Consider your answer carefully before setting pen to paper. You are challenged to argue about the extent to which you accept a verdict. Be sure that your answer will be clear to the examiner.

ⓔ There is no 'right way' of addressing this kind of question. You may decide to focus the first part of your discussion on the death of Stalin, and to consider why it might be considered 'the most important turning point', before challenging the proposition and presenting an alternative view, or not. The main thing to remember is that you have to discuss the entire period specified by the question, from 1917 to 1991. Arguably a chronological approach would be easiest in the limited time you have in the examination.

Student answer

I would not accept this verdict. Certainly the death of Stalin was significant for East–West relations — he had dominated the Soviet Union for more than two decades and oversaw the extension of Soviet power into the heart of Europe. Yet the fundamental priorities of Soviet foreign policy did not change significantly after his death. Arguably the end of the Second World War in 1945 was the most important turning point because it left the USSR as the arbiter of the fate of half of Europe for the next 44 years.

There were many turning points in the foreign policy relations between the Soviet Union and the western governments, starting with the Revolution of October 1917. The Bolsheviks introduced Marxist ideology into Russian foreign policy, thereby transforming European international relations. The Bolsheviks were convinced there would soon be a 'World Revolution' that would overthrow the governments in the West. They issued the Decree on Peace (Nov. 1917) and signed the Treaty of Brest-Litovsk (March 1918) to help secure the Bolshevik regime until revolutions erupted elsewhere.

When revolutions failed to materialise, they supported communist insurgents in Finland, the Baltic states, Germany, Hungary and Italy. In March 1919 the Bolsheviks established Comintern to promote 'World Revolution' through mostly covert means. In August 1920 Lenin tried to use the Red Army to make Poland a 'red bridge' by which to spread communism into Europe. Western governments responded to the Bolshevik threat by intervening in the Russian Civil War against them. They did not fight the Red Army directly, however, and did not stop the Reds from winning the civil war by 1921. Churchill later regretted that the West failed to 'strangle Bolshevism at birth'.

A turning point in Soviet foreign policy was marked in 1921 when Lenin sought a rapprochement with the West. He realised that the expected 'World Revolution' was unlikely to materialise soon, and he needed access to western trade to bolster his NEP to rebuild Russia's shattered economy. Western governments' fear of the USSR had subsided after the Poles' defeat of the Red Army in 1920 and the failure of communist insurgencies elsewhere, but their hostility to the Bolsheviks persisted. Nonetheless, many reluctantly agreed to trade deals with the USSR to help address their own postwar economic difficulties. Germany alone responded enthusiastically by signing the Treaty of Rapello in 1922. The agreement focused on trade, but had secret military clauses too. It was important mostly for reducing the USSR's diplomatic isolation in Europe.

e The point that there were many turning points in Soviet–western relations is well made. Identifying the shift in Lenin's foreign policy illustrates that nicely.

The next decade and more was marked by continuity in relations between the USSR and the West, reflected in Chicherin's continuation in office as the Soviet Commissar for Foreign Affairs. Stalin's 'Socialism in one country' concentrated on domestic priorities, not on ideological ambitions. Stalin stated in 1931 that the Soviet economy was a hundred years behind the West — they had to catch up in ten 'or go under'. He was convinced that conflict with the West was inevitable. The Five Year Plans of his 'Second Revolution' focused on the 'sinews of war'.

Hitler's accession to power in Germany in 1933 marked a major turning point in European foreign relations, though it was a year before the Soviets fully appreciated the threat he posed. Stalin annotated a copy of *Mein Kampf* and recognised both Hitler's hatred of 'Judeo-Bolshevism' and his ambition to conquer *Lebensraum* in Russia. The Soviets responded by intensifying the FYPs and the build-up of the Red Army, and by seeking 'collective security' during Litvinov's time as Foreign Commissar. The USSR joined the League of Nations (1934), and formed alliances with France (1935) and Czechoslovakia (1935). Soviet efforts to form a 'Popular Front' against Germany failed, however, because so many democrats regarded communism, especially during the Stalinist 'Terror', as worse than Fascism.

Stalin recognised that the ideological divisions in Europe — between the democracies, Fascists and Soviets — facilitated German ambitions. He withdrew support for the Republicans in the Spanish Civil War in 1938 because it seemed that Soviet intervention was uniting the West against him. The exclusion of the USSR from the Munich Conference (Sept. 1938) suggested to Stalin that Britain and France were trying to divert Hitler eastwards. Hence, when his efforts to form an anti-German coalition failed in the summer of 1939, Stalin told his new Commissar for Foreign Affairs, Molotov, to sign the Nazi–Soviet Pact (August 1939).

The pact with Germany marked a major shift in European relations, but it was not a decisive turning point because for both sides it was a temporary expedient. For Hitler it was intended to give Germany a free hand in Poland. For Stalin it was meant to buy time to better prepare the USSR for an inevitable war. Nonetheless, the aftermath of the pact was important. While Hitler used it to impose his control over most of mainland Europe, Stalin annexed the Baltic states, half of Poland, and parts of Finland and Romania. Even when the Soviets were suffering their worst setbacks during the Great Patriotic War in October 1941, Stalin told Eden, Britain's Foreign Secretary, that he intended to keep the annexed territories after the war.

e The main developments of foreign affairs in Europe in the 1920s and 1930s are discussed, with consideration given to the reasons behind the shifts in policies, and an assessment given as to the question posed about the 'most important turning point'.

Hitler's declaration of war on the USA in December 1941 caused the USSR, USA and UK to form the Grand Alliance against Germany — another significant turning point in East–West relations. Yet the Alliance was riven by ideological divisions, made worse by the American and British failure to launch the 'second front' they repeatedly promised. Stalin believed that D-Day finally happened in June 1944 because Germany was on the verge of defeat and the western leaders were afraid that the Red Army would sweep across all of Europe. The Grand Alliance was an alliance of convenience held together only by hostility to Hitler. Once Hitler was dead it soon began to fall apart.

e The Grand Alliance is important for any essay on East–West relations because it stands out as a time when those relations ought to have been positive.

I would argue that the end of the Second World War in 1945 was the most important turning point in Soviet relations with the West. The Red Army occupied half of Europe and Stalin had signalled to Churchill his intention to exert 'influence' across the region. Both sides were keen to cooperate at first, however, in order to maintain stability in postwar Europe. Roosevelt promised financial credits to help rebuild the shattered Soviet Union. Hence Stalin was prepared to be flexible. He signed the Declaration on Liberated Europe, did not annex any territory beyond the borders of 1941, allowed elections to be held in eastern Europe and the formation of coalition governments (in which communists were given disproportionate power). The new American President, Harry Truman, however, insisted that the Soviets abide by the letter of the Declaration and relations between him and Stalin soon soured, as was very clear at the Potsdam Conference (July 1945).

American Orthodox historians, starting with George Kennan, blamed Stalin for the Cold War, though Revisionist historians placed a lot of the blame on Truman. Certainly, Stalin was determined to control eastern Europe as a buffer zone for Soviet security, and he made it communist 'by degrees'. He also expected 'World Revolution' across Germany and other parts of western Europe. To that extent he was expansionist in his expectations, and he encouraged insurgents in Greece, but he had no intentions of using the Red Army to spread communism in western Europe. On the other hand, the Truman administration's use of 'atomic diplomacy' to curb Soviet ambitions, and the withholding of financial credits, contributed to Cold War tensions. It was the American decision to give Marshall Aid (ERP) that prompted Stalin to tighten his control over eastern Europe through Cominform, while the Anglo-American decision to rebuild the West German economy prompted the

Berlin Blockade (1948/9). After the failure of the blockade, thanks mostly to the USA's commitment to the Truman Doctrine, the Soviets and the western governments were forced to accept that maintaining the status quo would be the top priority of their foreign policies in Europe.

(e) If you decide that 1953 was *not* the most important turning point, you must be able to present a strong case in favour of another 'turning point' being the most important.

The death of Stalin was not the most important turning point in East–West relations. Although the collective leadership that succeeded him, and then Khrushchev, were keen for a thaw in the Cold War and talked about 'peaceful coexistence', there was a great deal of continuity in foreign affairs in Europe after 1949. That is reflected in the fact that they again offered the 'Stalin Note' to resolve the German Question.

Despite the 'Spirit of Geneva', Khrushchev's fundamental aim of keeping control over eastern Europe for security and ideological reasons was the same as Stalin's. He was prepared to be flexible to a degree, as with Gomułka in Poland, but he crushed the Hungarian Uprising because it threatened to unravel Soviet/communist control across eastern Europe. On the western side too, a new American leader changed little. Despite Eisenhower's pre-election rhetoric about 'roll-back', he was content with containment. With both superpowers having hydrogen bombs, the policy of MAD made war too dangerous to contemplate. Hence, the Americans did nothing to help the Hungarians in 1956 and, despite criticism from Willy Brandt, mayor of West Berlin, nothing was done about the building of the Berlin Wall either. The same was true when Brezhnev used the Warsaw Pact to end the 'Prague Spring' in 1968.

The era of Détente saw a gradual lessening of tensions in European foreign relations. Brandt's *Ostpolitik* was a significant development in relations between the two Germanies, but the progress made was due in large part to the support of Washington and Moscow. Both sides seemed to resolve the German Question with the Quadripartite Protocol (1970). The Helsinki Accords (1975) were ratified by every European country, apart from Albania. SALT 1 (1972) promised progress in reducing the threat of a nuclear war. The division of Europe into two ideologies since the end of the Second World War seemed permanent. The Soviet intervention in Afghanistan in 1979, however, ended Détente and sparked off a 'Second Cold War'. It was an unexpected and dramatic turning point in East–West relations, but it was not the most important point.

What made 1979 so important was that it coincided with a collapse in oil prices, which had a huge impact on the Soviet economy. Once President Carter, and especially his successor President Reagan, invested massively in new weapons systems using the latest computer technology, the Soviets found that they could not compete in terms of money or technology. The one-sided arms race, combined with Reagan's fierce rhetoric, including his 'evil empire' speech, persuaded the aged Politburo that the USA was planning for war. Security concerns and economic crisis contributed to the deaths of Brezhnev, Andropov and Chernenko in 1982–85.

e Keep your focus on the question, and offer your judgement about the importance of what you consider to have been turning points other than that specified in the question.

> With hindsight it might seem that Mikhail Gorbachev becoming the Soviet leader was the most important turning point in Soviet–western relations in 1917–91. I disagree, however. Despite *perestroika*, *glasnost* and his support for greater freedom and democracy, Gorbachev was a Leninist who wanted to reform the Soviet system. He never meant to destroy it. In fact, in order to save it he strove to get the USSR out of the Cold War, through reaching agreement with the Americans for nuclear disarmament, reducing the Soviet Union's conventional forces, withdrawing from Afghanistan and, most remarkably, allowing the people of eastern Europe to decide their own destinies. Even so, he did not expect the 'Sinatra doctrine' to result in the total disappearance of communism in eastern Europe by Christmas 1989.
>
> For Gorbachev and US President Bush to be able to declare the end of the Cold War in December 1989 was one of the most historic occasions in postwar European history. No one knew at the time that two years later, on Christmas Day 1991, the USSR itself would disappear. Economic collapse and rising nationalism, especially Russian nationalism under Boris Yeltsin, would undermine the Soviet system irreparably some time before the Soviet flag was replaced over the Kremlin by the Russian tricolour.

e No matter how pressed you are for time, make sure that you offer a conclusion. It should tally with the argument you outlined in your introduction.

> My conclusion is that despite the death of Stalin marking the end of an era inside the USSR, and allowing for a thaw in East–West relations, it was not the most important turning point in relations between the Soviet Union and western governments in 1917–91. There was a change of tone in East–West relations but the fundamental divide between the two ideological camps remained the same, and the two sides were content with the status quo for fear of MAD. Arguably the end of the Second World War in 1945 was the most important turning point because it left the Soviets in control of half of Europe, and they kept that control until shortly after the fall of the Berlin Wall in 1989.

e This sample essay ought to achieve a top grade since it addresses the question directly, deploys relevant and precise historical knowledge, shows deep understanding of the subject, and offers a well-substantiated conclusion.

Knowledge check answers

1 Though Russia was big in size and population, its economic underdevelopment meant that it was not as strong as one might otherwise have expected.

2 With one-third of Russia's exports passing through the Dardanelles, or Turkish Straits, they were vital for Russia's economy.

3 The alliance system gave Russia powerful allies in case it was attacked, but any conflict between members of the two alliances had the potential to escalate into a that would war involve all of Europe.

4 The Bolsheviks posed a military threat by means of the Red Army, but also, more insidiously, by encouraging communist insurgents to foment revolutions in western states.

5 If Karl Marx was correct, Germany had been ripe for revolution long ago. Its strong economy and large proletariat was expected to support communism in less developed countries like Russia.

6 Lenin sacrificed a great proportion of the Russian population, including most of its proletariat, in order to hold on to power over the rest of Russia.

7 The Bolsheviks hesitated to allow Comintern to act aggressively against western states for fear that their governments might respond by attacking the USSR with determination.

8 France supported the Poles in order to stop the spread of communism outside of Russia.

9 The Treaty of Rapello broke the diplomatic isolation of the USSR and ensured that the western governments did not unite against it. It also resulted in useful trade deals with Germany and in a transfer of military technologies and tactics to the Red Army.

10 'World Revolution' was by definition expansionary, but was also defensive as the leading Bolsheviks were concerned that the survival of the Russian revolution depended on it being bolstered by more advanced countries under communist control.

11 Churchill was referring specifically to the appalling suffering inflicted on the Russians in the civil war.

12 Western intervention was ineffective because western armies did not fight the Red Army directly, since people across Europe were war-weary.

13 Western governments responded positively to the Soviets' requests for peaceful coexistence because their fear of the USSR and communist insurgents had subsided and because postwar economic problems were a more pressing problem by 1921.

14 The countries that signed the Litvinov Protocol were all on the borders of the USSR.

15 Stalin recognised the threat posed by Hitler because the latter's hatred of communism and his ambitions for Lebensraum in Russia were explicitly stated in Mein Kampf.

16 The 'Terror' made Stalin's USSR seem far more dangerous than Hitler's Germany, until the invasion of Poland in 1939.

17 The fact that Britain and France made a deal with Germany and Italy, and excluded the Soviet Union from the proceedings, fully exposed Litvinov's failure to achieve 'collective security'.

18 The Soviets' decision to make a pact with Germany was shaped by the realisation that Britain and France would not make a pact with the USSR, and in any case Britain's military weakness raised doubts about the value of a pact with the West.

19 Despite the existence of Soviet plans to invade Europe in 1941, there is evidence to suggest that they were drawn up without Stalin's approval.

20 The accelerated build-up of the Red Army after the Nazi–Soviet Pact reflects Stalin's distrust of Hitler.

21 The American and British supplies to the USSR formed a small fraction of what the Red Army needed in the war against Germany, and Stalin regarded them as a very poor substitute for the 'second front' the Allies had promised him.

22 The Red Army had tried to conquer Poland in 1920, and the Poles were concerned that it would exploit any opportunity to conquer their country again.

23 Through cooperation with the West after the war, Stalin hoped for postwar stability and western economic aid in return.

24 Stalin believed that he had fulfilled his promises by not annexing eastern Europe and by allowing elections to be held and coalition governments to be formed.

25 Marxist ideology convinced Stalin that conflict was inevitable between communists and capitalists.

26 East–West conflict was highly probable after Germany's defeat because it was only the need to fight Nazi Germany that allowed the two ideological camps temporarily to set their differences aside.

27 The ERP took up 10 per cent of the US federal government's budget over a number of years from 1948.

28 Khrushchev cut spending on conventional military forces, but contradictorily he increased spending on nuclear weapons.

29 Khrushchev's fundamental foreign policy aims and priorities (the security of the USSR and the maintenance of Soviet control over eastern Europe) were the same as Stalin's.

30 Khrushchev believed that he had no choice but to crush the 'Hungarian Uprising', otherwise Soviet power and communist ideology would disappear across eastern Europe and Khrushchev himself could have been ousted by his rivals in the Politburo.

31 Khrushchev's attempts to negotiate a solution to the Berlin crisis were unsuccessful because the Americans were happy to exploit the Soviets' difficulties for Cold War propaganda.

32 It was partly a matter of the two systems competing for prestige, but the Space Race also raised the possibility of one side gaining a great advantage over the other in the Cold War by being able to deploy nuclear weapons in space.

33 Candidates for the American presidency emphasised their anti-communist credentials in order to portray themselves as strong, and also to appeal to the anti-communist sentiments prevailing among the American public.

34 Many people in eastern Europe were dissatisfied because their living standards were falling further and further behind those enjoyed in the West.

35 The heyday of the USSR might be considered a mirage because it coincided with a time of temporary weakness in the USA.

36 President Johnson's nonchalance about Czechoslovakia was because his primary concern was Vietnam, and there was nothing substantial he could have done about the Czechs.

37 As a Pole, Brzezinski was understandably hostile to the USSR and the communist system it had imposed on Poland.

38 Americans were so troubled by the Red Army's intervention in Afghanistan because they were worried that it threatened the USA's vital supplies of oil in the Middle East.

39 The Red Army's intervention in Afghanistan killed Détente, but only because it seemed to confirm growing concerns that the USSR had taken advantage of Détente to strengthen its position around the world at the USA's expense.

40 Western European governments were too dependent on the USA in NATO for their security to risk antagonising the American president by voicing their concerns in public.

41 The collapse in oil prices was catastrophic for the USSR since it greatly diminished its export earnings and thus its government finances.

42 Gorbachev's reduction of the Soviet Union's military strength was inspired partly by the need to save money, but more importantly by his desire to prove his sincerity in wanting to see an end to the Cold War.

43 President Yeltsin was such a formidable rival for Gorbachev because he enjoyed a popular electoral mandate, whereas Gorbachev had none.

44 The USSR could not compete with the USA in the arms race initiated by President Reagan because it lacked both the economic resources, and the technology, to do so.

Index

Note: **bold** page numbers indicate where definitions of key terms are to be found. Dates following names refer to time in office.

Index